Jilted Generation

Mixed Generation

Jilted Generation

How Britain Has Bankrupted its Youth

Ed Howker and Shiv Malik

ICON BOOKS

Published in the UK in 2010 by
Icon Books Ltd, Omnibus Business Centre,
39–41 North Road, London N7 9DP
email: info@iconbooks.co.uk
www.iconbooks.co.uk

Sold in the UK, Europe, South Africa and Asia
by Faber & Faber Ltd, Bloomsbury House,
74–77 Great Russell Street,
London WC1B 3DA or their agents

Distributed in the UK, Europe, South Africa and Asia
by TBS Ltd, TBS Distribution Centre, Colchester Road,
Frating Green, Colchester CO7 7DW

Published in Australia in 2010
by Allen & Unwin Pty Ltd,
PO Box 8500, 83 Alexander Street,
Crows Nest, NSW 2065

Distributed in Canada by
Penguin Books Canada,
90 Eglinton Avenue East, Suite 700,
Toronto, Ontario M4P 2YE

This edition published in the USA in 2010 by Totem Books
Inquiries to: Icon Books Ltd, Omnibus Business Centre,
39–41 North Road, London N7 9DP, UK

Distributed to the trade in the USA
by Consortium Book Sales and Distribution,
The Keg House, 34 Thirteenth Avenue NE, Suite 101,
Minneapolis, Minnesota 55413-1007

ISBN: 978-184831-198-5

Typeset in Plantin Light by Marie Doherty

Printed and bound in the UK by
CPI Mackays, Chatham ME5 8TD

CONTENTS

About the authors

Ed Howker is a journalist at *The Spectator* magazine and before that worked on current affairs documentaries for Channel 4's *Dispatches* programme. **Shiv Malik** writes for the *Sunday Times* and *Prospect* magazine and is a regular broadcaster. They are both 29 and live in London.

To our parents, thank you.

INTRODUCTION

Like all demographic change, the decline in childbirth carries both plusses and minuses. The crime rate ought to fall, since the 16–19 age-group includes the highest number of offenders; but that may be offset by a falling off in young recruits for the police. The young will suddenly find themselves much more sought-after. Universities and other places of higher education may be forced to lower their standards of entry. Employers will have to compete for them: the blight of youth unemployment should start to lift. Their wages, which in recent years have been falling behind, may accordingly burgeon.

'When the springs of youth run dry', leading article, *The Guardian*, 6 April 1988

Perhaps this is a book about coincidence, an unconnected series of unfortunate events. Human nature is such that we seek out simple shapes and narratives for our lives where there are none; we try to impose order on happenstance and accident. We look for heroes and villains. Stories comfort us. They give us someone to blame.

If nothing else, you could say that coincidence is painted thick onto the lives of those born in September 1979 and afterwards. Theirs would be the first generation to receive student loans and be compelled to pay tuition fees while their contemporaries, born just weeks earlier, and who therefore entered school a full year beforehand, would pay nothing. That they would start their university careers in the very year when property prices began their skyrocketing trajectory far beyond the future incomes of Britain's young workers seems unlucky. And that they will spend the next 30 years of their working lives paying off implicit government debt, and the very explicit deficit, seems somehow ill-fated too. And this, of course, assumes that they get a job, since many of them are joining the employment market following the worst recession in decades.

But what if these observations, many of which seem to be the concerns of the best-educated and richest young people, barely scratch the surface of the peculiar predicament in which an entire generation now find themselves? What if their disparate problems are linked and are getting worse? And what if the forces that shape their lives and their hardships – real or imagined – have been gathering pace and power for several decades so subtly that they are almost imperceptible today? Sometimes the only retort that seems to make sense is the one their parents offer: stop whingeing, stop complaining, just get on with it.

These, more or less, are the questions that have shaped this book, but to answer them fully is an almost impossible task. The post-79 generation have already lived through an era of momentous change. A 'Cold War' between Britain, its allies, and communism melted away before the oldest of them were teenagers, only to be replaced by unpredictable but frequent real wars in the Middle East and Asia. By the time that generation took GCSEs, the internet was beginning to change for ever the terms and opportunities for communication. And over the course of their lives digital innovations have led a rapid evolution in the means of manufacturing, service provision, and the nature and frequency of human interaction. Further, a political and scientific movement embryonic at their birth had pushed environmental concerns to the forefront of people's lives by the time they reached adulthood. It's all but impossible to measure the effect of so many complex forces on an entire generation's lives. So, we're just a page into this book and already we're forced to admit that it's not going to tell the whole story. For example, in the following pages we don't examine environmental issues in any detail. We don't trace the cause of feminism and try to quantify its effect on the freedoms and opportunities of women; we don't examine fully the impact of technology on the lives of young people, or even what numerous irregular and often contradictory education reforms have meant for them. Others have explored these trends better than we ever could. We don't even have a particular qualification for investigating this subject, apart from the fact that we're members of that post-79 generation.

So what are we looking at? This book examines four basic areas that form the foundation of people's lives regardless of which generation they're born into: Housing, Jobs, Inheritance – how wealth is transferred between generations – and Politics. There's another good reason for confining the terms of this book to these areas. These four subjects are easier to compare between generations, and we're going to need to do that if we're to establish whether Britain's young adults really are having an unexpectedly rough time. After that, we've tried to piece together what has happened and what can be done to fix it.

As you might have guessed from the title, we don't think our generation have been treated very well. We think they've been jilted – cast aside. What we tell in this book is a tale of neglect – not by our parents' generation (if anything, they've often been left to pick up the pieces), but by British society more generally. Perhaps that sounds strange. Believe us when we tell you that the story is about to get a whole lot stranger. But before we dive deep into the weirdness we'd better explain exactly who the jilted generation are.

Meet the jilted generation

The most recent measure of Britain's population comes from 2008. Figure 1 shows us the shape of those generations alive today.

The spike at the far right-hand side is a crude lumping together of everyone over the age of 90. Working leftwards, the next spike – occurring between the ages of 56 and 63 – shows the 'first-wave baby boom'. This spike occurred in

Figure 1. Population by age, 2008 (Office for National Statistics, principal population projections).

all Western countries following the end of the Second World War. There was a return to the stability of peacetime and soldiers came home from battle. Men and women got physical. So physical, in fact, that the matrons working for Britain's newly nationalised health service could barely cope with the number of new births. In America that boom carried on for the next twenty years, but in Britain it slowed down, rising again only between the years 1956 and 1965 in the 'second-wave baby boom'. Since then some have died and others have migrated, but today in total there are 16.7 million baby boomers in Britain.

What about the jilted generation? The line we draw for our generation isn't completely arbitrary. We are the children of the baby boomers, the so-called 'boomer echo' – a smaller lump that begins in 1979 and continues until 1994 – and there are around 13 million of us. Between these two generations are 11 million members of the so-called 'Generation X'. It's worth stating at the get-go that all these generational divides are far from exact, and we're not going to pretend that there are too many similarities between members of each cohort.

Age of the aged

Of these three generations, the largest by far are baby boomers, and their sheer size has some wide-ranging implications for our society. Britain has an ageing population and this is creating a demographic trend that is completely new: the ratio between the old and the young is imbalanced. Figure 2 shows a second graph taken from government predictions, estimating what will happen in the next twenty years.

It's easy to think that Britain's birth-rate or immigration explain why the UK population is growing. However, it's clear from this graph that between 1971 and 2031 the main factor driving up the population is that people aren't dying at the age they once did. The population aged under 45 remains broadly stable. But as the population increase over that 60-year period hits 15 million, there are predicted to be 11.5 million extra people aged 45 or older. And, since there are so many baby boomers, Britain's elderly population will also increase dramatically. By 2040, there will be 10 million over-75s, while the ranks of the super-old, aged over 90, will increase by 390 per cent as the first-wave boomers try to make a century as fit as ever. Over in Whitehall, government

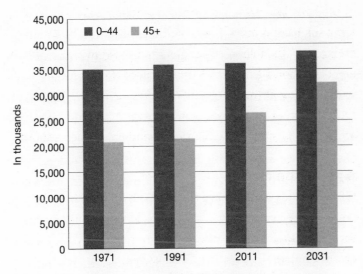

Figure 2. The balance of old and young in Britain, 1971–2031 (Office for National Statistics, principal population projections).

has been slowly waking up to the implications of all this. In 2009 a Treasury report on the generations warned:

> UK demographic developments … could potentially put direct pressure on the public finances through impacts on age-related expenditure, such as state pensions or health care. Demographic developments could also potentially have implications for the relative size of the workforce and economic growth, thereby indirectly affecting the public finances.[1]

In other words, Britain's ageing population could be storing up a whole heap of trouble for our generation who, in the forthcoming era of rising pension and healthcare costs, will be covering these costs on their behalf. What's more, there will be fewer of us working, so we'll have to pay proportionally more of our income in tax. Besides rising pension and healthcare costs, it's easy to think of a few more effects that the ageing population might have: as people get older they're unlikely to give up ownership of businesses and assets that might naturally have flowed down to younger generations in earlier times. Our economy might begin to skew a bit more directly towards older people's interests and buying habits. We shouldn't resent this. The Rolling Stones reached number one in the UK album chart yet again in 2010. We're getting used to it in the charts – we should be aware of the effect elsewhere.

But one of the most interesting aspects of population trends is that we haven't been aware of them. That's odd: broad demographics are fairly easy to predict – you know that if you have a great deal of children in one year, you'll have a large number of pensioners 65 years later – but the consequences of the spikes and booms seem somehow to have been swept under the carpet. In the course of researching this book, we discovered something very interesting: the Treasury began publishing long-term public finance reports only in 2002. We don't know why the UK exchequer didn't do this earlier, but you get a sense of the severity of the situation they discovered from their very first report: 'One of the key challenges facing the Government is the ageing of the population', it said. 'This trend will have profound effects on Britain's society and economy over the coming decades.'[2]

Britain's professional civil servants are known for their diplomatic language and delicate phraseology, so when they use the term 'profound effects' you know something might be about to go horribly wrong.

Lifestyles of the poor and aimless

But actually this book isn't just about the forthcoming 'age of the aged' and those 'profound effects' lurking around the corner. What we're interested in is the way our generation are living right now: our employment prospects, the homes we return to when work is ended, how much tax we pay and what that tax is paying for – the rudimentary issues.

We wanted to understand why the unemployment rate for young people began to rise long before the recession – in 2005; why 25 per cent of 16–17-year-olds were out of school and out of work at the height of the last economic boom. We needed to know why young people are spending a greater proportion of their income on rents than at any time in the last 30 years, and why Britain could enjoy a decade-long surge in house prices while the number of young first-time buyers fell through the floor. We tried to appreciate why we're paying our taxes to service a national debt that's potentially five times bigger than Britain's Gross Domestic Product. And why, when Britain enjoyed the greatest boom in living memory, young people's wages stagnated while the rest of the population's soared.

It turns out you don't have to cast your view forward to 2031 to get a sense of the severity of the jilted generation's predicament. And even more curiously, these difficulties are shaping not just our lives but those of our contemporaries across the developed world. The Organisation for Economic Co-operation and Development (OECD) finds that across the world's richest nations the young are more likely to be poor today than at any time in the last twenty years. There's a gathering sense, in fact, that our interests are being cast aside.

France's 2006 riots, in which Parisian students were teargassed by police for the first time since the late 1960s, came about for precisely this reason. One UK reporter on the scene, Angelique Chrisafis, described the chaos:

> The young rebels are fighting not for change but for the status quo – they want the same rights and benefits their parents enjoyed. They do not put flowers in their hair, but take to the streets with nooses round their necks, carrying mock gallows or coffins, chanting, 'We are disposable pieces of shit!'[3]

Germany's response to the issue has been somewhat more considered. They have set up a 'Foundation of the Rights of Future Generations' to address the problem of age-based wage disparities and the political exclusion of young people. And the issue is just beginning to gain momentum in the United States, where researchers have uncovered one statistic that says it all:

> Young men (aged twenty-five to thirty-four)
> with a high school degree or less earned about
> $4,000 less in 2002 than in 1975 (with earn-
> ings adjusted for inflation). Men with some
> college education also lost ground, earning
> about $3,500 a year less.[4]

This book doesn't examine the jilted generations in other countries, however. For one thing, the specific circumstances of any generation vary from one nation to the next. For another, while there has been plenty of discussion about 'baby boomers' and their legacy in Britain, no one has fully focused yet on the people really losing out: us.

The postponement of adulthood

The most pernicious aspect of young people's losing out is not material loss. It's unfortunate if young people have less money, but we're young – we can always earn more. The trouble is that by making employment and housing and taxation more difficult for young people to handle, a whole series of spin-off problems of a much more disturbing nature are created.

In the first place, these early imbalances create a kind of engine of inequality within our own generation. While young people from wealthy backgrounds are able to weather the tumult of their early years – they're supported through the bad jobs and high debts and expensive housing by their parents – the poorest have no means of escape. For too many of them, poverty and a lack of opportunity will therefore be further entrenched in their first years of adulthood.

There is another effect. Quite simply, young people aren't allowed to grow up. The postponement of adulthood doesn't refer to technological progress – our generation nearly all have iPods, computers and mobile phones. It doesn't represent young people's engagement with fashion or culture. Adulthood encompasses much more basic ideas: family, savings, community, realising ambitions and ideas, stability, even having children. And all these are connected by narratives – those vital stories humans construct for themselves.

As this book works through the home and employment markets, a powerful trend emerges of young people who have no narrative to piece together. We work in jobs and live in homes secured on short-term contracts; the steps of our lives are constantly meandering. We're not settled. Indeed, for many of us, only our childhood homes represent a fixed point, a permanent address, and so we return to them constantly and sometimes permanently. And all this holds back the start of our own lives, the forming of stable relationships and the mastering of our own destinies. Richard Sennett, the pre-eminent sociologist at the London School of Economics, has diagnosed the trend: 'The conditions of the new economy feed on experience which drifts in time, from place to place, from job to job',[5] he explains. He argues that getting jobs and sticking with them are vital to the 'adult experience'; but since so many young people are stuck working for agencies and in temporary posts, this doesn't happen.

Sennett opens his book *The Corrosion of Character* with the following dilemmas: 'How can long-term purposes be pursued in a short-term society? How can durable social relations be sustained? How can a human being develop a narrative of identity and life history in a society composed of episodes and fragments?'[6]

We don't ask them ourselves; rather, these are the questions loitering in the shadows, silently following each member of the jilted generation. Take, for example, the effect of over-priced housing. In 2009, 29 per cent of men and 18 per cent of women aged 20–34 were living with their parents.[7] Unsurprisingly, polling strongly suggests they find it difficult to form and maintain relationships at home. Polling also suggests that up to 2.8 million people aged between 18 and 44 are delaying children because they can't obtain affordable housing,[8] while 7 per cent of adults aged between 18 and 30 are delaying marriage because they can't afford to buy a home. That figure represents the equivalent of 385,000 couples – three times the number of marriages in a single year – postponing their wedding for want of somewhere affordable to live.[9]

Now consider the effect of unstable and poorly paid jobs. Not only do these make expensive housing even more unaffordable but they also come with their own implications. A 2005 study entitled 'Marriage and Globalisation' discovered that job instability has a massive effect on relationship formation in Britain. Women in part-time or contract work were around 60 per cent less likely to move in with their partner than women in permanent jobs. And while job stability had little effect on whether those women converted their relation-ships into marriage, employment had a big effect on men. As the authors found: 'Compared to those in permanent jobs, men in seasonal and casual jobs are 88 per cent less likely to convert their cohabitation into marriage and those on fixed-term contracts are 44 per cent less likely to do so.'[10]

It was once considered certain that couples in Britain had children later only because women chose to concentrate on their careers. Perhaps the relationship between work and income and housing and childbirth is different. It was deter-mined that couples chose to cohabit and marry later because they liked to 'play the field' or because the nature of modern relationships was hostile to long-term commitment. Things might be more complicated.

This book will argue that some of the observations we put down to short-term developments and fashions are actually the product of deeper, longer-term trends, and chief among these trends is the mechanism by which our society consid-ers the past and the future – our relationship with time. We believe that this relationship is dysfunctional, not because of 'the boomers' or because of the inherent nature of 'capitalism' but because of a way of thinking that has grown to dominate our public discourse and our conception of ourselves. It has left us unable to really join up the problems that the jilted generation now face, not because we're bad or purposefully selfish people, but simply because it never occurred to any of us to look. It's the reason why Britain has a pensions cri-sis, why we have huge debts and dislocated young people. It explains why Britain has been unable to equip for the fight the generation now joined in battle against poor public finances. It's why we're slowing the rate of childbirth just as our population grows to its oldest.

We can't see into the future, but these problems have been coming on for a lifetime. In 1991 a New Zealand academic named David Thomson wrote a book called *Selfish Generations?* In it, Thomson tried to guess the changes that would take place if the young continued to lose out in an otherwise flourishing society. There would be, he predicted: 'rising youth crime or suicide, homelessness, poor health care such as neglect of teeth, a reluctance to marry or undertake parental commitment, marriage breakdown, and mounting antipathy to all political processes'.[11] He certainly came closer to our generation's predicament than *The Guardian* did three years earlier in 1988. But to address the underlying concerns we must change our turn of thought, illuminate those shadows, consider looking again.

Slowly, sombrely, inevitably, the storm is gathering pace. Those 'profound effects' are waiting to be felt in full force. The generation who will bail Britain out can't quite get started. The generation waiting to retire are nervously looking on, wondering why. Meanwhile, the debts are getting bigger, jobs are getting scarcer, lives are getting tougher. If circumstances get worse, people will begin looking for simple shapes. They will start to seek out a narrative, any narrative. And then people will find someone to blame.

1

HOUSING

'I will extend opportunities to people who never had them before. As you know, we are building a property-owning democracy.'

Margaret Thatcher, interviewed in
Time magazine, 22 June 1987

'Over the Parliament our aim is to increase home ownership by one million and in particular help young families struggling to be first-time buyers.'

Tony Blair, speech to the Labour party conference, 27 September 2005

Starting at the top: owning a home

For decades now, politicians have been spoon-feeding British voters the same comforting message: home ownership is good – it helps build a 'stakeholder society' as Blair said, or a 'property-owning democracy' as both Thatcher and Cameron put it. Just before he became prime minister, Gordon Brown went even further: 'The problem is that even with the great ambitions of the 1950s or the 1980s, they did not succeed in widening the scope for home ownership to large numbers of people who want it', he told reporters. 'I would say a home-owning, asset-owning, wealth-owning democracy is what would be in the interests of our country because everybody would have a stake in the country.'[1]

Over the last 30 years there has been an observable change in the language, culture and attitudes of British people towards home-ownership, just as the politicians wanted. It's no longer something people aspire to – they view own-ing their own bricks and mortar as a right. Home-owning is counted by government as the primary mechanism by which people can save money throughout their lifetime, and as the best way to bind people into their communities and create a stable environment for children.

That stability could also be attained through the rental sector, as it is on the continent, but, as we'll see, the rules, regulations and costs that govern the rented sector have con-spired to ensure that tenants are always second-class citizens in our property-owning democracy.

If you're looking for some measure to show how intensely home-ownership has been hard-wired into Britain's national psyche, just look at Britain's prime-time TV slots, 'dinner-party conversations' and newspaper front pages. They are fascinated by it. It's a national obsession, but not one in which our generation can be involved. We can't afford it.

Part of the explanation we've received for being kept out of home-ownership is that Britain is in the middle of a 'housing crisis'. We all know that. The phrase is so ubiquitous that in the last decade it has appeared twice each day on average in one national publication or another.[2] We're told that there are many reasons for this crisis – a shortage of land, the growth in the buy-to-let market, the failure to build enough homes, and property speculation that has forced up their price. And in the meantime the jilted generation – the young – just happen to be left out. 'Hard luck. Sorry. Wait a few years and you'll be fine', everyone else might as well be saying.

If this 'crisis' forms one half of popular discussions about housing, the rest comes from the personal experience of Britain's opinion-formers and commentators. And, no surprises here, it's the jilted generation they have in their sights.

Scores of newspaper columnists have warned of the unhappy effect of 'boomerang kids' who return home to live with their parents after university on the household income. Others have exhorted parents to 'do the responsible thing' and 'kick out the KIPPERS' – 'Kids In Parents' Pockets Eroding Retirement Savings'.

We're told that we're freeloaders. And even acronyms created by sympathetic think-tanks to diagnose our problems in novel ways, like iPod – 'Insecure, Pressurised, Overtaxed and Debt-ridden' – are turned against us.

'Were these iPods', grumbled the columnist Giles Hattersley[3] in a *Times* article entitled 'The Indulged Generation', 'not the same lot who choose to study away from home, marry in their thirties and spend the decade their parents raised their children in, chasing dreams and drifting from career to career? How can it come as a surprise to any of them when they can't afford a house?' Concluding, Hattersley says that this peculiar acronym should be re-christened to reflect the true nature of our generation: 'Infantile Posse of Over-indulged Drunks'.[4]

We're told that all this is our fault. Our generation is seen as so feckless that there's even a BBC2 programme, *Bank of Mum and Dad*, in which 'grown-ups' concerned about their children's lifestyle perform the financial equivalent of an alcoholic's intervention to attempt to put them on the straight and narrow.

And just in case we might wheedle our way out of such criticism by pretending our circumstances are different, pre-eminent scientists like Kenan Malik are only too happy to explain: 'The idea that you [Britain's young people] are uniquely disadvantaged seems to be absurd.'[5]

In the following pages, we'll begin to present a rather different picture. We'll explain what's actually going on in the housing market, the facts behind how our parents' generation got their own houses – facts that have been conveniently swept under the carpet like an embarrassing family secret – and we'll try to pin down who and what is to blame for the disaster that is modern British housing.

Let's start with a no-brainer. Figure 3 shows that since 1949, house prices have, with the odd blip, risen fairly consistently. The graph isn't in 'real terms', so it's not adjusted for inflation (we'll come to that). What it shows is that if you bought for £1,911 – the average house price – in 1949, that

Figure 3. Average house prices since 1949 (Department of Communities and Local Government (DCLG), table 502).

house would have risen in value to £2,530 by 1960, and in 1990 the same house would be worth £60,000. Today it would be £226,064.

Gazing knowingly at these figures, perhaps the older generation can take some comfort that prices were cheaper twenty years before they bought their first house, just as they were cheaper in 1990 than now. They suffered the same trouble, they might argue. It's always been tough. And they might have a point – earning enough to buy your own home is a real struggle. People make sacrifices to do it. Earlier generations sacrificed to buy knowing that a stable home would be a good investment for their savings and their family. Now we, they argue, must sacrifice too – and what's more, we should quit whining about it like the 'over-indulged drunks' we are. But this graph masks the real facts.

Behind the curtains

If Britain's political leaders wanted to create that 'property-owning democracy', then critical to the project was ensuring that young people could get into the housing market quickly. And, twenty years ago, that seemed to be working out OK. In 1990, if you went around Britain knocking at every home, you would discover that 8 per cent of the owners were under the age of 25, and that 43 per cent were aged between 25 and 34. Young people, in other words, accounted for more than half of all home-owners. Repeat the experience twenty years later and what you find is a remarkable change: just 2 per cent of home-owners are under 25, and 27 per cent are aged 25–34.[6] And this change is far too large to be explained by demographics alone.

Now instead of going around to everyone's house, imagine going around to every single bank and building society and asking them who they've been giving mortgages to in the last twenty years. Figure 4 measures the age of mortgage borrowers during the greatest era of easy credit in history. As you can see, despite outrageous 90, 100 and even 125 per cent mortgage offers, the proportion of young people with mortgages fell for both the under-25s and the 25–34 group, from

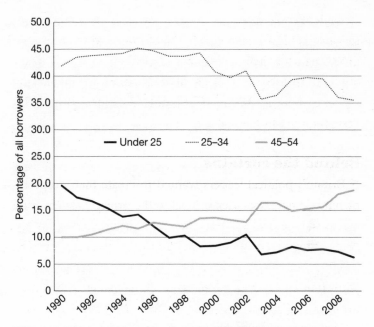

Figure 4. Mortgage borrowers by age, UK (DCLG, table 537).

around 62 per cent of total borrowers in 1990 to just under 42 per cent in 2009. Meanwhile, borrowers in the 45–54 age range have gone from making up 10 per cent of the mortgage market to 18.7 per cent.

If you narrow this picture of the total mortgage market right down to just those mortgages given out to first-time buyers, you can see a similar pattern. In 1990 under-25s made up 30 per cent of the first-time buyer market. By 2009, those first-timers made up just 15.9 per cent of the market. The rate halved. Meanwhile, in the demographic 25–34, there has been a gain in the number of buyers of around the same proportion. The facts are pretty conclusive: first-time buyers are buying later.

So why is this? The Council of Mortgage Lenders thinks it has something to do with lifestyle choices. 'More young people going to university and trends towards later marriage and child-bearing, mean that people are delaying their house purchase decisions.'[7]

It's a view shared by the government. In 2009, the Office for National Statistics' *Social Trends* survey stated: 'Various life-style changes may have contributed to this pattern [of ageing first-time buyers]. For example, people are now generally marrying later in life than they did ten years ago. In addition, more young people are going to university and some leave home to live in shared accommodation before setting up their own homes.'

It seems like a persuasive argument. Buying a house just isn't what young people do these days. But maybe something else is going on. While some of us may be genuinely waiting longer because we want to explore the options, most of us still want to own a house. When MORI conducted a poll of people aged under 25, 84 per cent responded that they would be likely to want to buy their own home within the next ten years.[8]

So, if we really want to own a home, is there another reason that would explain why our generation is waiting longer than ever to get in on the act? Of course there is. It's not just that homes have got more expensive, it's that they have become disproportionately expensive. Outrageously expensive. Expensive in ways that some people won't admit, and that the first graph in this chapter can't hope to express. We're going to need more graphs …

The data in Figure 5 is drawn from the government's own figures and, as you can see, represents more clearly than ever how our generation has been, and will continue to be, doinked.

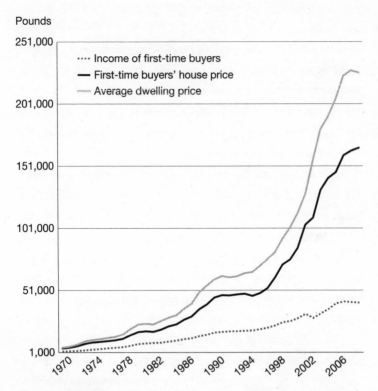

Figure 5. First-time buyers since the 1970s (UK house price and income data from DCLG).

The line that reaches the highest point represents the average price of a home in the UK. As you can see, costs have exploded in the last 40 years. If food costs had gone up as fast as house prices, a pint of milk would cost £2.43, a jar of coffee would cost £20.22, and a chicken would cost £47.50 (and that's a standard battery chicken, not an organic, sandal-wearing chicken).[9] To put it another way, if in 1970 you invested £4,975 – the average price of a house – into the housing market, you'd get back over £220,000 by 2009. If you put that money into a bank account that rose with the price of everything except housing – fuel, clothes, food, cars – you would receive around £50,000.

The next line down is the typical price that first-time buyers have been paying for a house over the same period. You would expect it to be below average because first-time buyers tend to start at the bottom of the housing ladder. Of course the wider the gap between the average price of a house and what a first-time buyer pays, the lower the standard of home those first-time buyers are likely to get. The gap between the two has been widening. In 1970, first-time buyers were getting houses costing 13 per cent less than the average. Today, their homes are 27 per cent less than the average. The bottom of the ladder has been moved even lower. (We come on to just how pitifully low in a few pages.) However, housing inflation, like all kinds of inflation, isn't a problem if wages also increase. As long as wages and prices remain roughly in proportion, then all this needn't be much of a problem.

The bottom line in our graph is the combined income of those first-time buyers and their partners. For us to get the same deal as those buying housing at the start of the 1970s, you would want the gap between the bottom line and the middle line – incomes and prices – to remain as small as possible over time. In fact, this gap has widened massively.

Figure 6 is the same graph with another line added.

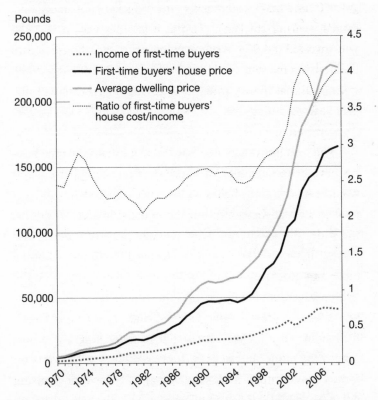

Figure 6. First-time buyers since the 1970s (showing ratio of first-time buyer house price to income).

The dotted line represents that ratio of first-time buyer house prices to incomes. What you see is that between 1970 and

1990 the ratio hovers around 2.42. This is the average multiple of what our parents' generation paid for their houses in their youth – i.e., they managed to get a roof over their head for 2.42 times their income. For our generation, the story is completely different. Between 1997 and 2009 this ratio was much larger, 3.41. And it's still climbing. Perhaps the difference between those ratios doesn't sound too bad? After all, what's a ratio point between generations?

Well, if first-time buyers in 2009 were to sacrifice what our parents sacrificed to get on the housing ladder, then the average first-time house wouldn't cost £165,500 but a little under £100,000. That's a huge difference in price. Multiply that by the thousands of first-timers who got on the ladder in 2009 and then total that figure up for every year since 1997 and you soon end up with a number in the billions.

Martin Weale, head of the National Institute of Economic and Social Research, got his team to look at the same problem but from a different angle. They estimated that if house prices had grown in line with the stock market over the last two decades (5 per cent per year), then average house prices would now be 50 per cent cheaper. They believe this should be the fair cost of housing. Anything higher than that leads to a skewed economy because those who already own houses stop investing in useful things like companies and business and start using their house like an ATM – an easy source of cash. Every time someone takes out a second mortgage or sells up, retires and downsizes, they take that over-inflated profit with them, even though they've done very little – or nothing – to earn it. So who pays the cost? The answer is simple: those entering the market for the first time. It's our generation who must pay the older generation that profit. So how much is this over-payment worth?

£1,300,000,000,000 (one trillion, three hundred billion).[10]

That's a nightmare figure, but could things be about to change? Britain had a recession in 2008 and 2009, house prices are falling, and we have the lowest interest rates in British history; so surely, after skyrocketing income/price ratios and an absurd decade-and-a-half housing bubble, now might be the time to buy? Wrong. The goal-posts have moved. Banks are wary of lending to all but those with the most established credit histories, and that's not us. In February 2009, the average deposit that banks demanded of first-time buyers reached 25 per cent – the highest since records began in 1974. The higher the deposit, the longer it takes to join the market. So even when prices are falling, our generation is still locked out.

This situation is bad. It's also new. The plain truth is that earlier generations enjoyed four clear advantages when affording a home that we simply don't have:

1: The secret tax break

Not so long ago, there was a principle that if you had a mortgage and you also paid tax, the chancellor of the day would allow you to claim tax relief on the interest part of the loan. The idea, which went back to the 19th century, was about fairness. A bank will make a profit by charging you interest on the money they lend you to buy your home. In turn they will pay tax on that profit. If the home-owner is taxed as well, the same transaction is being taxed twice. That's not fair. So before 1974, tax relief on mortgages, or 'MITA', was available to anyone who owned a home, regardless of the size of the loan.

In 1975, the Labour government placed a cap of £25,000 on the MITA; but, since the average house price was just £11,000, almost every house fell within the tax relief limit. In 1983, the system changed again when the Thatcher government increased the cap to £30,000 and introduced MIRAS, or Mortgage Interest Relief at Source. The MIRAS scheme enabled borrowers to get tax relief on mortgage interest that Britain's 1,200 banks, building societies, friendly societies and insurance companies administered on behalf of their lenders. You didn't even have to fill out the paperwork. The average price of a house was £26,500 in 1983 so, again, most could take advantage of the system. Better still, until 1988, married couples could combine their MIRAS allowances to £60,000.

In total the MIRAS giveaway alone helped 19 million people get on the housing ladder. In 1983 the subsidy cost the government £2.8bn. By 1990 it was costing the government £7.7bn. In today's money those subsidies would be £5.7bn and £14.1bn respectively. So what became of this massive housing subsidy?

After 1990, MIRAS was whittled away by the Major and Blair administrations before being formally abolished by Gordon Brown with effect from 6 April 2000. He called it a 'middle-class perk', which, given his comments about widening the scope of home-ownership, seems not a little opportunistic. And it's a £14bn subsidy that we won't see this year, or next, or ever – for one simple reason: it was abolished at the very moment we reached adulthood, the very moment we also wanted to think about signing up to the 'property-owning democracy', just as our politicians had encouraged us to do. More to the point, neither Brown nor his predecessors have really done anything to help the housing concerns of any class of our generation. This principle of tax relief on mortgages had existed for over a century. So for MIRAS to be scrapped now represents a failure to reciprocate. Simply put, while society has been happy to receive these benefits in the past, it has been unwilling to pass them on to us.

2: The sale of public housing

Described by the *Observer* as 'one of the most popular political promises in history' and by Michael Heseltine at the time as laying 'the foundations for one of the most important social revolutions of this century',[11] the 'right to buy' changed Britain for ever. Quite simply it was an advantage offered to a previous generation that allowed council tenants who had lived in their house for more than two years to stop paying rent to their council and start paying mortgages for their homes. Enacted in 1980, the scheme was both ideologically and electorally useful for Margaret Thatcher's administration – the most sincere move her government made towards the creation of that 'property-owning democracy' and an instant hit with the buyers who showed their support for her at the ballot box.

For Sir Gerald Kaufman, who ran Labour's house-building programme before the 1979 election, it 'certainly helped win them re-election in 1983. Many people then felt they owed the Conservative Party their vote.'[12]

This was true in some places more than others. One of the oddities of 'right to buy' was that it was the mechanism used for the single greatest piece of corruption in local government history. Tory Westminster Council leader and Tesco heiress Dame Shirley Porter used right to buy to ensure she remained in control of the council by moving Tory voters into marginal Westminster wards and Labour voters into wards with such strong majorities that their ballots would be unable to sway the election. When the scandal was finally exposed, she was ordered to repay £42m by Westminster's auditor.[13]

Across Britain, the effect of right to buy was even more dramatic. Between 1980 and 2009, 1.85 million formerly public homes were sold to their tenants in England, another 450,000 in Scotland: the biggest change to Britain's housing stock since the Blitz. Figure 7 shows how many council homes were sold each year.

However, it wasn't just the right to buy that empowered millions: the government gave a further incentive to purchase housing – they slashed the price. That meant that previous generations got a double advantage. Not only was there a glut of houses available for purchase, but they could buy those homes at between 60 and 40 per cent of their real value, depriving the exchequer of half the revenues they might otherwise have received in the open market.

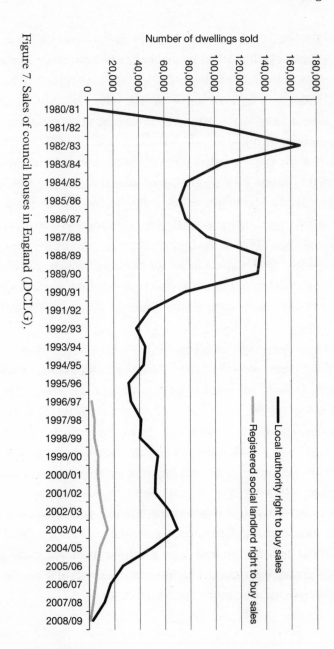

Figure 7. Sales of council houses in England (DCLG).

The scale and effect of right to buy has still not been properly understood – a process made more difficult because local councils didn't keep sufficiently detailed records – but marking the 30th anniversary of the scheme, HSBC tried to estimate the total worth of right to buy. Their figures are astounding.

For one thing, looking at the figures you realise that right to buy constitutes the single largest piece of privatisation ever attempted by the British government – larger, in fact, than all others (trains, water boards, electricity suppliers, airports) put together. HSBC estimate that the total cost of the housing stock sold was an almighty £85.74bn, of which the state received just £45.38bn. So the 'right to buy' generations were able to make a flat £40bn profit as soon as they got a mortgage.[14]

As you can see from Figure 7, it's not going to happen again any time soon. By 2008/09 only a few thousand council homes were being sold in England, while at the peak of the scheme more than 160,000 went. There are several reasons for this – the first, clearly, is that the recent recession has cut people's income and tightened credit. But more fundamentally, what was once an amazing deal was made much less attractive in 2003 when 41 local authorities took the decision to cap the discount at £16,000, while most others reduced the discounts they offered too (see table opposite). And, in 2004, the government tightened the rules even further, requiring tenants to have lived in their home for more than five years before qualifying.

Discounts falling on council house sales:[15]

1998/99	50%
1999/00	48%
2000/01	47%
2001/02	44%
2002/03	41%
2003/04	37%
2004/05	33%
2005/06	31%
2006/07	27%
2007/08	24%
2008/09	24%

It's a little ironic that just one year later Tony Blair referred to right to buy in his speech to the Labour party conference, saying: 'Twenty years ago we gifted the ground of aspiration to the Tories. Today we've got it back and we'll never yield it up to them again.'[16]

In truth, the ground on the issue of council house sales simply had to be 'yielded up', as the prime minister knew full well. Figure 8 shows the scale of the advantage gained by previous generations. If you divide the revenue that councils get per house by the number of sales and then adjust for inflation, you get, for the first time, some sense of the scale of that advantage. The higher the graph gets, the worse the deal that buyers get.

As you can see, by 2005, the prospect of buying a council house had never looked less appealing, and things have only

Pounds

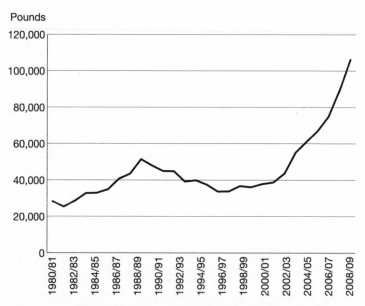

Figure 8. Government receipts per council house sale (2008 prices). (Note: these figures relate to England only, but the situation is very similar for the rest of the UK.) (HSBC and DCLG)

got worse. Contrary to what both Labour and Conservative parties have admitted, the right to buy scheme has been administered in the most irresponsible way possible – causing maximum damage to those desperate for reasonable housing today: neither party replaced the housing stock.

There are lots of arguments for and against the provision of housing by the state, but let's put those to one side for the moment and concentrate on the hard numbers. In the last 30 years, unlike the state provision of benefits, or health and education, capital government spending on housing has dropped like a brick. Between 1974 and 1989, spending fell by two thirds in real terms.[17] Inevitably this translated into a steep fall in the numbers of new houses being completed by local authorities – 86 per cent fewer public homes were built in 1989 than in 1974.[18] And since then the trend has continued. Peter Malpass is the Professor of Housing Studies at the University of the West of England. His specialism is public housing, and he says: 'In the period 1980/81 to 2001/02 public housing was cut by 64 per cent, while all other main welfare programmes saw positive growth.'[19]

In total, Britain has sold off half of its public housing stock – with several serious consequences, including the ever-swelling waiting lists for council housing that thwart so many vulnerable people's life chances in our society. However, most directly, the scarcity of the product pushes up the value of those that remain. So, as council homes were sold and their stock not replenished, their value rose. What this means for our generation is remarkably simple. Those wonderful deals that underpinned Thatcher's electoral success can never be repeated. Once again our generation seems locked out.

3: The public house-building programme

If a glut pushes down the value of a product and scarcity pushes it back up, and this holds good for public housing, it also works for the entire housing market: so no prizes for guessing what has happened in the last 30 years. Figure 9 is another graph (sorry, there aren't too many more) – and as you can see, things have gone horribly wrong since around 1983.

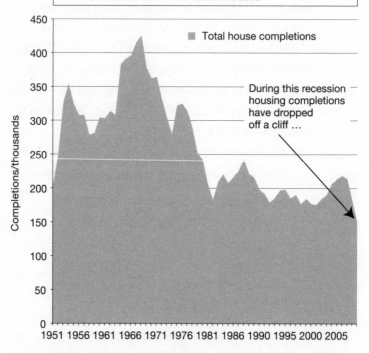

Boomer average house builds 1951–1984: 308,000 per year.
Jilted average house builds 1998-2009: 191,000 per year.
That is a difference of 1.44 million houses.

Total house completions

During this recession housing completions have dropped off a cliff ...

Figure 9. Total UK house completions since 1951 (Office of the Deputy Prime Minister; National Assembly for Wales; Scottish Executive; Department of the Environment, Northern Ireland).

But look what happened before that. When our parents' generation were reaching the age at which they would consider buying a house things were easy. The generation before them, rebuilding Britain following the horrors of the Second World War, ensured that they had somewhere to live. There were plenty of houses and, as a result, houses were cheap; but then, in the early 1980s – right when the houses that we might move into should have been built – there was a steep decline in production. It's as if the boomer generation just forgot. To understand why, we need to give this graph a makeover.

Look at Figure 10 – after the makeover – where we break down who is building these houses. The message is clear: in the late 1970s, government stops building and the private sector simply doesn't make up the shortfall. What's more, when recessions hit in the 1980s and the late 2000s, private building drops to levels not seen since the early 1950s – when Britain was still recovering from a war for national survival. In

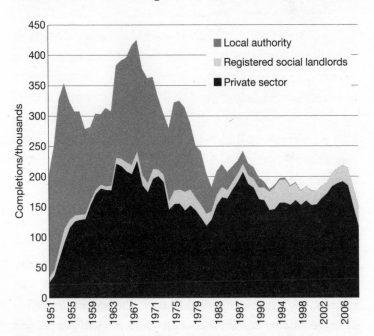

Figure 10. UK house completions by sector since 1951. (Note: completions for 2009 partially estimated for Scotland, Wales and Northern Ireland.) (DCLG)

1968, 425,000 houses were erected. By 2008, in the midst of our 'housing crisis', just 182,700 were built. In 2010, house-builders expect the fewest houses to be built in the UK for a century.[20]

Why? One explanation is the incompetent asset management of Britain's main builders, who bought land at the height of its value before the crash and are now unable to develop on it until prices rise again, since they won't make a profit. But even those developers who invested wisely will gain little from building and selling homes now, when they can do so in a few years when prices rise. They have an inbuilt profit interest in ensuring that housing remains scarce.

For Avner Offer, Chichele Professor of Economic History at All Souls, Oxford, Britain's approach to housing provision has been plain irresponsible: 'From the late 1960s onwards, construction fell below the GDP trend, down to a level of absolute provision so low that it had not been seen since the 1890s.' Offer notes that the retreat of the state and the concentration of house-building power in the private sector had one obvious consequence: '[T]he main outcome was a decisive retreat from prudential provision.'[21]

The sheer scale of the failure is remarkable. You are more likely to live in a house built between 1851 and 1918 – when the UK population was 30 million – than in the last 25 years, in which time our population has doubled. And the situation is hardly likely to change any time soon. In 2007, the Labour government's Comprehensive Spending Review stated that by 2016, Britain would be building 240,000 homes per annum. At the time, the target seemed ambitious.

Case study: John Prescott's solution to the housing crisis

Back in February 2005, the former deputy prime minister John Prescott pronounced that he had solved Britain's housing crisis in one brilliant move: 'This is a house that can meet the needs of people who can't afford a house at the moment with all the energy and water efficiency savings, environment, good building standards.'

He was referring to the final design of the so-called 'Summit House', a project to build affordable housing for the 21st century that would cost just £60,000. The first of the design was rolled out in a place called Allerton Bywater in Yorkshire. Prescott broke the ground on the new development and declared: 'Now that £60,000 house which some of them said you can't do I launched it in Manchester, at an exhibition. I'm absolutely delighted about it.'

In total, 23 were built in Yorkshire but they went on sale in 2007 for, er, £225,000. Prescott's grasp of housing was so poor that he seemed not to realise that the major cost in the purchase of a home is not the bricks and mortar but the land. And even the build cost of his new homes – £60,000 – was three times more expensive than many private sector new-build properties. He had solved nothing.

Today, it looks ridiculous. As Figure 9 shows, Britain is building less now than in 1951.

4: Getting more for their money

Given that in the last 30 years people's incomes have increased
by two or three times, you might expect houses to have got
bigger too – TVs certainly did – but that hasn't happened. In
fact, the hands-off approach that left private developers with
the responsibility to build Britain out of the housing shortage
has had other negative effects. It turns out that the free market
has failed to build homes of high quality that are suitable for
the needs of future generations. Once again, the advantages
enjoyed by older generations are not available to us.

Both tenants and residents of social housing built from the
late 1960s until 1980 could be certain that their homes were
large and well-built, because the government said they must
be – by law. In 1961 Sir Parker Morris led a committee to
design a set of minimum criteria for good housing construction, design, and facilities. They wrote these up in the report
'Homes for Today and Tomorrow', and the standards were
recommended by the Ministry of Housing to local authority
builders first. Then, in 1967 they became mandatory for all
housing built in new towns. In 1969, the Parker Morris standard was extended to all council housing. But the standards
were not to last. By the early 1980s, they had been abandoned
completely following the Conservatives' 1980 Housing and
Local Government Act. Morris's advice was considered out-
dated and too expensive.

The chances are that we will never see this kind of regulation again. Recent attempts by the Blair and Brown governments' Homes and Communities quango to bring back 'Parker Morris + 10' standards – for 10 per cent larger homes – have been mired in farce. Early in 2010, a study by housing consultants HATC found that nearly nine out of ten private homes built in the south-east failed to meet these basic 'safety net' standards. The worst were actually one third smaller. So Britain remains the only country in Western Europe to lack minimum housing standards. And it shows. As the table below demonstrates, the housing now being built in the UK is considerably smaller than before:

Comparison of dwelling sizes[22]

A = floor space (m^2); B = number of rooms; C = room size (m^2)

	All dwellings			*Newly-built dwellings*		
	A	B	C	A	B	C
UK	85	5.2	16.3	76	4.8	15.8
Germany	86.7	4.4	19.7	109.2	5.1	21.4
France	88	3.9	22.6	112.8	4.2	26.9

We're in a weird little club – every other European country save Britain, Italy and Luxembourg has produced larger housing in the last twenty years. In his recent paper for the think-tank Policy Exchange, Professor Alan Evans of the University of Reading Business School is withering: 'The standard of housing in Britain has fallen substantially relative to the rest of Western Europe. Britain has the oldest, pokiest housing.'[23]

And that is what our generation, who will not benefit from basic housing standard regulations, will find most available.

Since the Parker Morris standards applied predominantly to public building, their demise does not offer a comprehensive explanation for this trend, however. For that, you need look at what has actually been built. We know far fewer homes have been erected, with the obvious effect that Britain's housing stock is getting older and more expensive to maintain, and tends to be energy-inefficient. We also know our homes are smaller by room numbers. Figure 11 shows just how much smaller. In the last ten years, there has been an explosion in the number of one- and two-bedroom properties built.

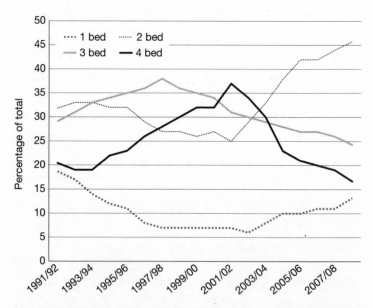

Figure 11. House completions by bedroom since 1991 (England). (DCLG, table 254)

What's more, homes have also become more tightly packed together – more dense. In 2007, new dwellings in England were built at an average of 44 per hectare, compared with 41 in 2006 and 26 in 1991. The east of England and the East Midlands had the lowest density of newly-built homes, at 35 and 37 dwellings per hectare respectively. Although London had the highest density of new homes of any English region, at 76 dwellings per hectare, this was a decrease of 28 per cent on 2005, when the density of new homes was 106 per hectare.[24]

All this means that Britain is building more flats. A lot more flats. There's good reason to believe that this will have significant social costs, which will be explained later in this chapter. First, Figure 12 shows what has happened.

This trend is very strange. In the first place, people don't want to live in flats. Period. In a March 2005 MORI poll, 50 per cent of those questioned favoured a detached house and 22 per cent a bungalow. Just 2 per cent wanted a low-rise flat and 1 per cent a flat in a high-rise block,[25] and there's no reason to believe these numbers are going to change.

Psychologically, houses feel bigger; they tend to be better for raising a family; and they usually, if not always, come with outside space, which is highly desirable. That's why they are more expensive.

The second strangeness follows on: given that the housing market has been completely dominated by private builders, you might expect them to be building what people actually want to live in. After all, in a free market, business tries to satisfy the demands of the customer. But in this case customers

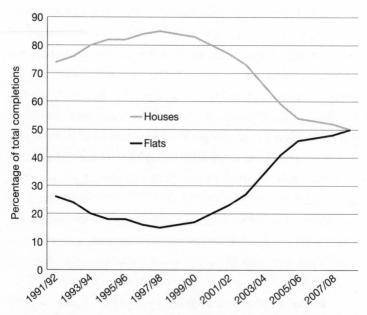

Figure 12. Flats or houses? Completions since 1991 (England). (DCLG, table 254)

are obviously not getting what they want. This is one of those 'Get Alan Greenspan on the line and ask him what the @#!? is going on with the free market!' moments.

Well, you don't have to ask the former chairman of the US Federal Reserve – it's pretty straightforward. In the recent history of British housing, the buyer and the consumer haven't been the same person. Builders haven't been building what residents want. They've been building what housing speculators want. And those speculators haven't been living in the homes, they've been renting them out. As a result, our generation is in big trouble.

Speculators or 'buy-to-letters' have been egged on by TV programmes like *Property Ladder* and thousands of newspaper articles, magazine features and investment advisors persuading them that with the right portfolio mix they too can become property millionaires. In the last six years, 647,000 homes have been bought by 'buy-to-let' investors who hope that poorer people than they will rent them.[26]

So who are these speculators? And why have they been making a bad situation worse? Well, the answer is they're all around us. We know them quite well – they're our parents' generation. By 2008, 58 per cent of buy-to-let investors were baby-boomers aged 46–65. Only 3.5 per cent were over 65. Only 2 per cent were under 26. In fact, from 2004 to 2008 the average age of a buy-to-let investor has gone from 42 to 48.[27] There's an obvious reason for this. In order to invest, you need to have both a stable income and ready access to credit. And thanks to the myriad advantages that previous generations have received, they're much more likely to have both.

To give you a flavour of just how blind Britain's politicians are to the damaging effect of buy-to-let on Britain's house-building, you need only check out the consultation paper offered by the Labour party in the run-up to the 2010 general election, proposing to cut stamp duty for buy-to-let investors. This just adds insult to the serious injuries suffered by Britain's young people.

What's more, evidence unearthed by the housing pressure group Priced Out shows that our former prime minister Gordon Brown knew perfectly well the effect of buy-to-let on first-time buyers. In fact, a paper was commissioned by Tony

Blair while Gordon was still chancellor in 2004. It told both men that first-time buyers were being crowded out from the housing market by the buy-to-letters:

> The falling numbers of new entrants has not had the expected cooling effect on the housing market as the growing trend of buy-to-let may have taken up much of the slack ... The increase in activity may have the effect of crowding out FTBs as, typically, rental properties and those being sought by FTBs often have the same characteristics.[28]

So the chancellor knew, the prime minister knew. Guess what they did. Nothing. In later chapters we'll offer a few ideas about why that was, but the point here is very straightforward: Britain's older population got tax breaks for mortgages, better homes and more of them than we did. So we have to live differently.

According to David Salusbury, chairman of the National Landlords' Association (NLA), buy-to-let performs a vital service: 'The 20,000 landlords that I represent at the NLA are providing real social benefits in their housing provision for other people.'[29]

What's more, when our parents' generation, those 'buy-to-letters', bought second or even third homes, they weren't just doing good: they truly believed that by becoming landlords they could enhance their pensions, retire early or just get rich. What no one said is that one group more than any other would be filling the pension pots and helping the old to retire – Britain's young people. In this way, buy-to-let has become yet another mechanism by which wealth has been transferred from the young to the old, for the very simple reason that our generation is doing the renting.

The way we live now

Everyone has to live somewhere. Aside from Britain's 150,000 legally defined homeless and 400,000 hidden homeless – those sleeping in bed and breakfasts or refuges, or sofa-surfing with friends[30] – there are broadly speaking only three types of accommodation available: owning your house, renting from local authorities and social landlords, or renting from private landlords. Under-35s make up 20 per cent of all tenures in Britain and so, straightforwardly, if everything were equal across generations you would expect to see under-35s living in 20 per cent of the owner-occupied homes, 20 per cent of the socially-rented homes and 20 per cent of privately-rented homes. As we know, as you get older you acquire more wealth, so you might expect to see few young people on the housing ladder and more living in rented accommodation than homes they own themselves. And in fact they do: just 13 per cent of owner-occupied homes are owned by people under 35. Given that, you might expect to see vastly more young people in both the social and private rented sectors.

Unfortunately, that's not what the figures say: social renting is only doing its fair share – just 21 per cent of social tenants are under the age of 35. The reason is simply capacity. Millions of council houses have been sold off, and as a result waiting lists have rocketed from 1 million to 1.7 million in the last ten years – and that doesn't include anyone in the system waiting for a better home. Travel down to your local council's housing office and you'll quickly see the effects of this: tearful mothers desperate to be re-housed; seven-person families living in two- and three-bedroom flats; and pensioners isolated in tower blocks. In short, there are millions of people waiting for the state to help them begin their future.

Case study: Newham – a lifetime of waiting

The London borough of Newham has the second-worst council-house waiting list in the whole country (first place belongs to Sheffield City). Thirty per cent of families are waiting to get into their first council property (Sheffield is 43 per cent), and with demand like that, people have to wait a long time. As Newham councillor Paul Shafer explains: 'There's been two major problems over the last 30 years. The first was right to buy, and the second is that the Tory government never let us have the money to build more houses. Newham sold 10,000 houses out of a stock of 30,000. That didn't have to be a problem but then Labour never reversed the situation. They left it too late and since then we were never allowed to borrow from the banks, and we had no way to find the money to build more houses.' So now, he explains, the wait for a four-bedroom house is at least fifteen years, and the wait for a three-bed is over eight years.

Single mother Claudia Neolide, 29, has been patiently waiting for a flat for four years, so that she and her twelve-year-old son can move into somewhere more affordable. At the moment she is paying over £1,000 a month for a two-bedroom flat. After paying her rent, she has just £200 left for the rest of the month for her and her son. 'That means that there isn't much to save. And it's difficult to go out, or think of having a holiday. The cost of housing is so expensive.' The worst part is that she's been told she will probably have to wait another six years before she gets somewhere affordable to live.

Even before he left school, Maruf Deen, 23, from Stratford seemed to know that leaving home would be hard. He put his name on the list for a one-bedroom flat when he was sixteen. Seven years later he's still waiting. He should be doing well. Deen got a 2:1 degree in business management from Greenwich University, and though it took him twelve months, last year he finally found a job working at the reception of the local council office. He now earns £17,000 a year. But it's not enough to allow him to move out from home, where he lives with his parents and ten others in a four-bedroom house. 'If I moved out, it would cost me £200 a week in rent. When you add in the cost of living and council tax, it's just too expensive.' In fact now he's employed, he doesn't think he'll ever get out of his parents' absurdly overcrowded home. 'The council houses go to those people in need: the unemployed, those on benefits, but that's unfair because it means that if you work, if you're working-class, you don't get a house. I guess it's just the way the system works.'

Everyone else is waiting to begin their future too, and they're doing it in the only other place they can to avoid moving back in with their parents – renting in the private sector. Private renting is dominated by tenants from our generation – under-35s make up 52 per cent of them, as the table below demonstrates.

Private renting by age spread percentage[31]

Under 35	52
35–44	21
45–64	17
65 or over	9
Total	**100**

This is a disproportionately large figure, but is it an exceptional one? After all, some might argue that you should expect young people to need the flexibility that private renting gives; that they needed it in the 1960s and 1970s too; that it has always been this way. It hasn't.

The facts are difficult to come by. For one thing, many records don't exist; for another, the ones that do are hard to compare directly. There are, however, some striking pieces of evidence that the housing situation of our parents was very different. When the Council of Mortgage Lenders actually asked older people about their living arrangements in their early years, they found some startling differences between the generations. While 52–55 per cent of people aged 45–65 rented their first property when they first left home in their twenties, 74 per cent of those aged 18–24 are renting their first property now – half of them in the private sector.[32]

Some might say that the dramatic increase in university entrants explains this trend – students require short-term rents, and there are more students. But the real bulge in private renting has occurred in young people between the ages of 25 and 34, after university. This age group makes up 33.3 per cent of renters in the UK (44.1 per cent in London)[33].

Something has definitely changed, and it seems to have changed in the last ten years – exactly the point at which the buy-to-let market exploded – with the number of young households (under the age of 30) living in privately rented properties rising from around 30 per cent in 1997 to 49 per cent in 2009.[34]

Quite simply, young people in Britain today have been caught and trapped. In 2005, the Joseph Rowntree Foundation concluded that there were 1.25 million, mainly young, people in Britain who were too rich to get council housing but too poor to afford a mortgage on the cheapest houses in their area. The Foundation estimated that nearly 60,000 new households enter this trap every year. So much for that 'property-owning democracy' we've heard so much about. It's a situation that, 40 years ago, would have been unthinkable, when there was a glut of housing and cheap prices. In fact, in 1971 the Housing Research Foundation found that there were more than 1 million people who rented but could actually afford to buy. We've had a stark reversal of generational fortunes: 1 million members of an older generation who could choose, 1.2 million members of a younger generation who cannot.

Still, is renting really that bad? Speak to David Salusbury of the NLA for a few minutes and you'd certainly think not. Early in 2010, he explained that 'the last decade has seen 1 million more renters who like the choice, the ease and the flexibility which renting brings. Like most things, if you asked people individually they would probably say renting was the perfect option for them at a number of points in their life.'[35]

That sounds great! So, is renting really that good? No. Mr Salusbury is making really bad excuses for the buy-to-let cash-in. He's on the winning side of a relationship between tenants and landlords that isn't just unfair, it's completely dysfunctional.

So, let's just give a few home truths about the state of private rented homes and their tenants. In the first place, far from being 'the perfect option', the 2009 English Housing Survey showed that private renters have the lowest housing satisfaction rate of any householders: 'Overall satisfaction with current accommodation varied by tenure, with more than two-thirds (68 per cent) of owner-occupiers in England saying they were very satisfied with their homes in 2007/08, compared with around half of social and private renters (49 per cent and 47 per cent respectively).'[36]

It's easy to see why. Private rented accommodation is the least likely to be energy-efficient, the most likely of all tenure types to fail at least one of the four decent homes criteria – 45 per cent is rated as non-decent.[37] What's more, to get poor-quality private rented accommodation up to scratch would cost around £8,530 per home. So it's no surprise that many private landlords simply don't bother.

If, as Mr Salusbury states, '1 million more renters […] like the choice, the ease and the flexibility which renting brings', they're putting up with some shoddy housing to get those advantages.

Second, given that the product landlords are providing is so inferior, you might expect it to be cheap. Fat chance. Let's examine social renting – renting from the council or a housing association – first. In terms of money outlay, social renting is a good deal: tenants are better protected and it's much, much cheaper. In 2007/08, for example, the average monthly rent in the social sector was £369 per month, while the average in the private sector was £589 or 62 per cent more.

That sounds like a bad deal, but it's actually even worse than you think. The cost of private renting is completely unaffordable. In fact, private renters are more likely to spend higher proportions of their income on housing costs than even those with a mortgage. Figure 13 gives a breakdown of what it looks like.

The truth is that the much-vaunted 'flexibility' about which David Salusbury and the rest of the buy-to-let gang talk so fondly is a red herring. People in the private rented sector are paying more for an inferior product, and at least 1.2 million of them have no alternative.

There are two reasons why people are forced into private renting: because they can't afford to buy homes of their own – they've been crowded out by buy-to-letters in a highly constrained market – and because of the impoverished state of the social housing sector. However, to understand why the private rented sector has managed to create such bad and

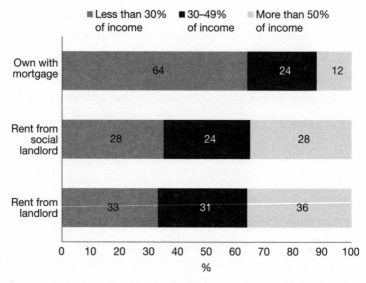

Figure 13. Proportion of household income spent on housing costs by tenure. 'Don't know' responses have been excluded. (YouGov, 2009)

expensive housing, we've got to understand what has happened while previous generations have been in charge of Britain. Once again, they had a whole series of advantages that we don't have.

The government originally got involved in making rules for the private sector during the First World War. While men were off fighting the Germans in France, women were providing desperately needed labour in munitions factories. However, the government didn't want landlords to take advantage of this extra household income by putting up rents during wartime. So rent levels were controlled. It was the first example of the philosophy of tenant rights that reached its peak in the 1960s and 1970s when government gave tenants the right to have their rents assessed by officers of the local rent committee. They would gauge the fairness of the rent compared to the local area, even giving discounts in neighbourhoods where supply was constrained. The barrage of rental legislation passed in that period also gave paying tenants, and not landlords, the right to determine how long they remained in their home.

In the 1980s the Conservative government decided that this regulation of the private rented sector had gone too far. Landlords complained that if they were unable to hike up rents, or evict their tenants to find better-paying ones, it was no longer worth being a landlord. In 1988, Margaret Thatcher introduced a new Housing Act designed to deregulate the private rented housing market, and created the 'Assured Tenancy' contract. For tenants it was anything but assured: landlords were now able to determine the time limit that tenants could live in their property, and in future rents would not be 'fair' – i.e. not assessed by rent control officers – but they would be set by the market. In fact, the government even claimed that 'market rents' would get cheaper, since the market would take account of the lack of security in the contract. Here's what the Act said:

> The major change proposed to the shorthold regime is that ... the rent will not be at a fair rent level but at a market level that takes account of the limited degree of contractual security which the tenant has been offered.[38]

In fact, it would take a further deregulation of the private rental market before landlords would get interested again. In 1996 the Major government switched the default rental contract from 'assured' to 'assured shorthold', which gave tenants just six months of security before the landlord could politely ask them to leave (throw them out) or put up the rent.

All these moves were designed to change the philosophy of how people rented. For our parents, renting meant paying for residence in a home they happened not to own in name. For our generation, renting allows us to hire a space to live in before we're asked to move on again.

The statistics reveal this shift. In 1988, 58 per cent of tenancies in the private sector were regulated, and just under half had registered rent. Twenty years later, that regulated figure had plummeted to 4.3 per cent. Today just 1.8 per cent are registered.[39] All other forms of renting have declined. Meanwhile, an extra 1 million shorthold tenancies have appeared in England.[40] Most of this growth appears after 2000, and the reality is that most of the people living in rented accommodation don't live in one place for long – in fact, 40 per cent move on before one year, and 70 per cent after staying less than three years. The median stay is 1.7 years in private renting; and this compares with 7.1 years for those with mortgages and 7.8 for those living in the social sector. The effect has been to turn our generation into migrants in our own country.

The Thatcher government's confident prediction that 'market rates' would keep rental costs down has also proved wrong. We're now paying more for less contractual security.

We're living in homes that are of worse quality than council housing. We're signing short contracts with landlords who have fewer qualifications than guys who flip burgers in McDonald's, and we're paying a higher proportion of our income to live in our homes than those with mortgages. What's more, there are two groups who continue to profit from this: the government, who have shamelessly avoided any increase in council house-building and so don't have to subsidise our accommodation as they did earlier generations; and all those buy-to-letters whose mortgages we're now paying. Young people seem to be in the wrong place at the wrong time: Britain today.

Let's play consequences

It's already clear that the last 30 years of housing policy, the free market, the buy-to-let boom, the removal of public housing provision and house-buying incentives, together with the fall in house-building, have taken their toll on our generation. But so far we've analysed only the economic consequences. It's the often unexamined social costs that exact the highest price for all of us.

Let's start at home. At the beginning of this chapter, we quoted some of the slang terms used to describe our generation: 'Kids in Parents' Pockets Eroding Retirement Savings' – Kippers, Boomerang Kids, iPods, drunks. What they're getting at is the idea that our generation are completely dependent on their parents.

In 2009, 29 per cent of men aged 20–34 were living with their parents, as were 18 per cent of women. These are huge numbers, the highest for generations: 2.9 million young people. And not all of these young people were saving for mortgage deposits – 45 per cent, according to recent research, can't afford to move out.[41] What many commentators ignore is that, saddled with debt and, as we'll see in the next chapter, pitiful employment prospects, it's unsurprising that millions are clinging to their family homes for stability. To claim that this is somehow what young people want is absurd. You need only ask the MP for Newquay (see opposite).

Indeed, living with parents is damaging our lives. A Shelter report published in 2010 found that 58 per cent of 18–34-year-old people living with their parents find it difficult to hold down a relationship.[42] And you can understand that this makes it even harder for them to move out, since a ready solution to high housing costs is to share accommodation. But there are more dramatic consequences too. The effect on the 2.1 million young men living with their parents, for example, extends far beyond the front door.

In 2009, research by Queen Mary, University of London found that stay-at-home sons are more violent than those who move out – responsible, in fact, for 16 per cent of all violent injuries caused in the previous year.[43] According to Professor Jeremy Coid of Queen Mary's forensic psychiatry research unit: 'Violence outside of the home, mainly involving strangers, is the most common scenario and just one of a series of hedonistic and negative social behaviours such as hazardous drinking, drug misuse, sexual risk taking, and non-violent antisocial behaviour. And these are more common among young men who do not have responsibilities of

Case study: the MP who lives with his mum and dad

The difficulty in affording stable accommodation is now so acute that in 2010 Britain elected Steve Gilbert, the 33-year-old Liberal Democrat MP for St Austell and Newquay, who can't afford to buy a house in his constituency, so he still lives with his parents. Mr Gilbert was raised in the area and attended the local state school. Most of the people he grew up with are suffering from the same problem.

'The housing ladder is just not there for the local population around Newquay', he explains. 'And not only have young people been priced out of the housing market but reasonably well-paid jobs are hard to come by. In my constituency, the cheapest house prices can be twelve to fourteen times the average wage, and there's a queue a mile long for council housing. It's like a generation contract has broken down. There's just no provision for this.

'Thousands of people cannot afford a place to live in the communities in which they grew up. We've flipped back to an age of massive boundaries – it's just the ones we have now are very different. My concern is that this will get worse as the government is forced to make cuts. We need to give young people a way out of living at home.'

providing their own accommodation, supporting dependent children, or experiencing beneficial effects on their behaviour from living with a female partner.'[44]

His report concludes: 'The persisting high prevalence of violence among young adult men is explained by delay in moving to social independence.' In this way, changes in Britain's housing settlement have exacted a devastating social cost. But there's more. Much more.

Take the move to reduce home sizes by builders eager to make a profit, and who remain unregulated. Add to this the severe shortage of council housing in the UK, and what you discover is that Britain contains plenty of unhappy families. In *Full House?*, another Shelter report on family housing, 77 per cent of respondents strongly agreed that overcrowding had a negative effect on family relationships. And the five effects of overcrowding with the highest level of strong agreement were as follows:

> 'Little privacy in our home' – 92 per cent
> Depression, anxiety or stress – 86 per cent
> Not enough room for children to play
>   – 84 per cent
> Children argue and fight – 81 per cent
> Sleep disturbance – 75 per cent[45]

Imagine how these families feel. Imagine what effect all this has on teachers and grades, colleagues and employment prospects. The consequence of high house prices is also that 1.5 million adults say they are unable to look after their elderly parents because they can't afford to live near them, and so place them in care. And, in turn, 1.5 million grandparents say they are missing out on helping to take care of their grandchildren because their own children can't afford to live close by. That's an agonising legacy for 30 years of housing policy. But if Britain's housing policies are damaging the relationships of families today, they may have an even more dramatic effect: actually stopping families from being created tomorrow.

Right at the start of this chapter we quoted the Council of Mortgage Lenders and the government. They both thought that young people were moving away from home-ownership out of choice and that this might also be linked to other life-style trends. As the government's own *Social Trends* survey put it: 'Various life-style changes may have contributed to this pattern [of ageing first-time buyers]. For example, people are now generally marrying later in life than they did ten years ago.'

We know that marriage rates are at their lowest for 150 years. We also know that couples, married or not, are having children later than ever before. Are these all simultaneous free choices born out of new ways of living? Or perhaps we've misunderstood how people settle down and raise families? Perhaps we've got this causal relationship backwards, and people delay having children and settling down exactly because they don't have any stability about where they live?

It turns out that this is the case. Poll after poll reveals that people place huge significance on having a home of their own. And a recent set of polls find that home-ownership and stability dictate decisions like starting a family. One survey in Shelter's 2010 report *The Human Cost* found that 2.8 million people aged 18 to 44 admit they're delaying having children because of a lack of affordable housing available to them. Of them, 19 per cent are delaying for as long as six years, and over a third expect housing costs to continue to delay their plans for another four years.

That poll also found that 40 per cent say their current home is too small for children (small wonder when we've been building so many one- and two-bedroom flats), while 37 per cent say that their current housing costs mean they can't afford to have children – and these statistics are highest for those renting privately. Shelter states: 'Having a settled and secure home life is a key consideration when deciding to start a family and this result may reflect the lack of certainty that many private renters feel, as they know they may be asked by their landlord to move out and look for another property.'

Another more recent poll found that four in ten young adults have said they will not settle down until they can buy their own house, and some have actually delayed marriage because of it.[46] Fifty per cent of renters believe that they will not be able to buy a home in their local area.[47] And these are more than existential fears. The average income recorded for first-time buyers is £40,971 and the average cost of the house they buy is £165,512. Today, that gives an income-to-house-price ratio of 4.04. Home-buyers are sacrificing nearly 80 per cent more than their parents so that an older generation can have a better standard of living. In 1957 the cost of housing made up 9 per cent of people's average expenditure. Now it makes up 19 per cent. Costs have more than doubled,[48] and if these costs are, in turn, linked to finding love, getting married, having children, raising them properly, and even the

very safety of our communities, our generation has every reason to be miserable about its prospects. Those who accuse us
of 'whining' have completely missed the point.

Conclusion: the estate we're in

Housing is society's fundamental building block. It's completely defining. Housing is not just a traded commodity, not
a mere space in which people reside, but a focal point for the
narrative of their lives, providing shelter, security, a bedrock
of certainty in an uncertain world. And there are huge costs to
society and its success if we get housing wrong.

In Britain today, it's beyond doubt that we are getting it
wrong; that the housing we build is unsuitable and the way we
divide that housing between us is unreasonable. It's beyond
doubt that we're making it more difficult for people to find
housing that is permanent. We're placing insurmountable
barriers in the way of the success of young people, those who
will fashion our society and reproduce the next generation to
live in it.

Some among us are fortunate enough to have parents
who will bail us out. They will 'drain their retirement funds'
to stump up for a deposit or even subsidise the rent. We can't
resent these transfers of wealth when parents only want to see
their children settled in a home of their own. Yet the effect of
these beneficent acts will be to further entrench inequality in
our society and to stifle social mobility within our own generation. How severe this effect will be, we don't know. How
much resentment will be stored up, we can only imagine.

All this has happened, not because our society has a death wish, but because it never properly examined the future. The theme of this book, in many ways, is that recent generations seemed to forget completely that the future exists, selling off the legacies of even earlier generations for profit now, and selling off our future for a fast buck to feed the demands of yesterday. It was easy money, since the people who bear the costs were not around to defend themselves. Well, we're here now. The future has a canny way of arriving just when you should expect it.

2

JOBS

'I grew up in the '30s with an unemployed father. He didn't riot. He got on his bike and looked for work, and he kept looking 'til he found it.'

> Norman Tebbit, Conservative party conference speech, 1981 (response to a speech by a young Tory who suggested that the Brixton and Birmingham riots were a natural response to rising unemployment)

'If I was watching this I'd throw something at the TV and say get off your backsides and work and we should cut all your benefits and starve you into going back to work.'

> Lord Digby Jones, *Panorama*, BBC1, April 2010 (response on meeting two middle-class unemployed young men after they admitted they claimed £12,000 benefits each year and as a result didn't need to find work)

Some things never change. There's a 30-year gap between these two statements from the former Tory employment secretary Norman Tebbit and the ex-Labour trade minister Digby Jones, and yet both men are saying the same thing – explicitly they're urging unemployed young people to find work, implicitly criticising them as cheats, too lazy to get a job while the rest of the hard-working population subsidises their existence. But if the sentiment is the same, they're saying it in two completely different ways. Tebbit summons an image of his father in an attempt to root his criticism in the traditional morality of the family (a similar technique was used by Gordon Brown in the 2010 election campaign; he could barely open his mouth without disgorging himself of the 'values' he learned from his dad, John Ebenezer Brown). Jones's comment, meanwhile, is even more hard-hitting. While recording an edition of the BBC current affairs programme *Panorama*, he angrily told two unemployed young men that they should be starved into work – clearly not an inducement the portly Lord Jones looks to have experienced himself.

Few things seem to irritate these men and thousands of like-minded people more than 'benefit scroungers', those who could work but choose not to. Historically, they have been called the 'undeserving poor' and have attracted the criticism and contempt of, predominantly, rich and old men, not just in the last 30, but for hundreds of years. They are a vital part of Britain's national conversation – journalists like Charles Dickens and Henry Mayhew went in search of them in the Victorian era; and earlier still, the Poor Law Amendment Act of 1834 was specifically designed to 'root out' the Georgian equivalent of 'benefits scroungers' and force them into work, either by Jones's method – starvation – or by the horrors of the workhouse.

While there has been no reintroduction of the workhouse into British society, nor widespread starvation, there's something curiously Victorian about the employment prospects and work status of the jilted generation: Victorian because, like the working class of that era, we're accused of profligacy and can't seem to save our money; because our jobs are poorly-paid, unstable and difficult to come by. More than anything else we're vulnerable, and yet the attitude of much of society towards us is that we're lazy and undeserving. This opinion is Victorian in another sense too – as we shall see, it's sickeningly hypocritical.

There is, as you may now expect, an acronym to sum up the position of Britain's most languid young people: NEETs – 'Not in Education, Employment or Training' – and, as the following curious extract from Conservative writer Michael Portillo demonstrates, genuine moral outrage associated with their situation: '[Benefits] should help people through misfortunes, not subsidise slobbery. They should go to the deserving, not the undeserving. They should pull people up, not push them down ... perhaps, at least, we ought to assume that fit young people are not entitled to anything. If a few young men from sink estates are now heroes in Afghanistan, why should we presume that all the others are capable of nothing useful at all?'[1]

But it's really not the case that Britain's streets are packed with lazy young people indulged by a profligate Labour government. Reading Mr Portillo you can't help but get the impression that he simply has no clue about the severity of the challenges faced by our generation, about the crippling debt, the poor work prospects and the benefits trap that are now the essential characteristics of our working experience. Visit the suburbs, towns and inner cities of Britain and you find a generation flatly betrayed by those who built the society in which they flounder. That some have grown lazy and good-for-nothing-but-benefits is really the least of the problems, however: others have turned to crime, some to suicide.

The crisis they could no longer ignore

A funeral cortège proceeded from Vicky Harrison's home in Blackburn, Lancashire on Wednesday 14 April to Darwen Masonic Hall. No longer sanctified, the gothic former Congregationalist church still hosts ceremonies for the dead of the district as it did in the 19th and 20th centuries. Architecture just like it litters the towns of the north of England, stone-cut testament to the severity and religiosity of long-dead generations of mill-workers and churchgoers. But there was nothing old-fashioned about the circumstances of Vicky Harrison's life or her death.

Antonia Victoria Harrison was found by her father slumped in a chair, surrounded by emptied blister-packs of pills. An intelligent and determined girl, she had been meticulous about her own death, writing three final letters – to her mother, father and boyfriend – before she ended her own life. 'Please don't be sad', she said. 'It is not your fault. I want everybody in my life to be HAPPY. It is just that I don't want to be me anymore.'

Those are very final words. Vicky had reached a startling and uncomfortable conclusion for any person – not least a beautiful, clever young woman. 'I don't want to be me anymore' is not a phrase that invites an easy retort, even an easy explanation. Her father didn't call her 'vulnerable' – quite the opposite. He said she had a 'stunning smile', that she was 'bright'. Her defining characteristic was, he said, 'determination'.

It's impossible to ever truly know the motivation for self-harm or the trigger for suicide, but it's possible to get a sense of contributing factors. Vicky Harrison was depressed for all kinds of reasons but, among these, her father singles out one: aged 21, with ten good GCSEs and three respectable A-levels, his daughter was still waiting for her life to start. She had applied for more than 200 jobs since she returned home to Blackburn from university – she'd written covering letters and filled in applications for positions as a receptionist, in administration, as a junior TV producer, a temp, even a dinner lady. She had worked hard, she had been determined. She did everything right, everything we're told to do at school and by our parents, but she was still waiting. So, on the day before she was forced to sign on to receive unemployment benefits, she gave up and sat down to write letters for the final time.

'There was no reason why she shouldn't have been able to find a job', said her father in the days that followed. 'What upsets us so much is that there are obviously so many other people out there in a similar position.'

With these words, Mr Harrison ensured that the short life and untimely death of his daughter became a cause célèbre for youth unemployment. Her death was reported across Europe, clear evidence that the recession was hitting young people harder than anyone expected.

That Britain's recession has been 'deep', as economists say, or 'really dreadful', as they actually mean, is beyond dispute. The number of people receiving unemployment benefits jumped by 68 per cent in 2009 – more quickly than at any time since the 1950s. And, as this figure implies, the job prospects of Britain's young workers have been eviscerated. At the time of writing, 60 per cent of all those unemployed in Britain are drawn from the jilted generation – 1.5 million people. And the situation is worst of all for the very young: for young people aged 25–34 the unemployment rate is nearly one in ten; for young people like Vicky Harrison, aged 18–24, the rate is nearly one in five. The rate for those aged 16–17 is 35.1 per cent – more than one in three.[2] These stats may look bad, but viewed in the context of what has happened to other age groups, they're almost incomprehensible. The same survey of unemployment from which they were drawn shows that the rate for people aged between 50 and the retirement age is just 5.1 per cent. Men over the age of 60 actually found more work during the recession, while the stand-out winners were women of the same age. The proportion of the female workforce aged over 60 actually increased by 2 per cent in that time. There's a blatant iniquity here: while the young are experiencing the highest unemployment rates in modern British history, our parents' generation are actually doing better than when the recession began.

According to David Blanchflower, who oversaw a report by The Prince's Trust into youth employment, the reason that young people were particularly damaged by the downturn is simple: 'Firms have just simply stopped hiring', he said. 'Even graduates have gone down the spiral and taken the less [demanding] jobs. And, it has pushed the people at the bottom out of work. I expect we shall see an increasingly depressed and debilitated generation who, as a result, become decreasingly likely to find work and hang on to it.'[3]

When, in December 2009, record unemployment figures were released, the Labour employment minister Jim Knight was keen to show how seriously he was taking the situation: 'We know from the recessions of the '80s and '90s that long-term unemployment can affect young people not just while they are out of work but for many years to come.'[4]

If these words showed that the minister wasn't complacent, they were also designed to be misleading by suggesting that the current recession was similar to the previous one in terms of its impact on young people's job prospects: but it's quite different. Seventeen years ago, Britain was at the height of the 1990s recession. There were 3 million unemployed, but, demographically speaking, the proportions were much more evenly spread across the generations. Twenty per cent of 16–17-year-olds – 15 per cent less than now – were unemployed, as were 9.6 per cent of people aged over 50 – twice as many as today. So this recession is much worse for young people, and there's a simple reason for the discrepancy that

Mr Knight refused to admit. Even before young people got hammered by the latest recession, many of them were out of work already.

While Britain's Gross Domestic Product (GDP) per capita rose more quickly than that of any other G7 country in the last decade, two strange things happened. Just as older people seemed to gain more work in the recession, their numbers within the workforce had been rising for the ten years before it. A little-known survey by National Statistics found that not only did the total number of workers between the ages of 50 and retirement age rise by 225,000, but they also took good jobs.[5]

Similarly, the downward trend in young people's employment during the recession was also a continuation of a much longer depression. Figure 14 shows what happened.

Far from age being a barrier to entry into the workforce, the exact opposite seems to be true: the older you are, the less likely you are to be unemployed. As for the job prospects of 16–17-year-olds, these don't even correspond to economic upswings and downswings as the others seem to – over time they just get worse and worse. Just before the recession began, one third of 16–17-year-olds were not in work. It's absurd to suggest that they're all lazy representatives of the 'undeserving poor'. Their working lives have barely begun, and even if it's possible to make a case for welfare dependency in older age groups, can that really mean that teenagers should be disregarded in this way too? To do so is to write off an entire generation. So, something else must be going on.

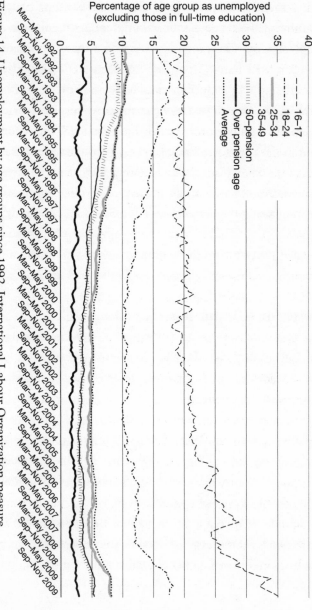

Figure 14. Unemployment by age groups since 1992, International Labour Organization measure. (Note: percentages exclude those in full-time education.)

The truth is that the jilted generation are the first lab-rats in a decades-long economic experiment. As the figures above imply, we can already be confident that the experiment isn't going so well. Plenty of the lab-rats seem to be falling behind, but what exactly is the experiment meant to prove? Politicians from all parties tell us that we're the new recruits for the 'globalised economy' or the 'knowledge economy'. This economy, they say, is based on 'flexible labour', 'transferable skills', and 'innovative working practices'. What they really mean by all this waffle isn't easy to understand. You might even suspect them of being deliberately obscure. So, to know exactly what this experiment is and what the results might be, we're going to have to start from the beginning, when the people who set it up were, like us, beginning to join the workforce.

Jobs for all and jobs for life

In most critical respects the nature of work has changed so fundamentally since Portillo, Jones and Tebbit were young that it's no surprise they're slow to recognise the change – but things really are different.

To start with, the kind of job prospects our generation have today are completely different from the ones they found on entering the workforce. Between 1945 and 1976 unemployment never rose above 3 per cent of the working population. So work was never difficult to obtain, and were those three men to have got on their bikes, they would have found work quickly. Since 1976, however, unemployment has never really fallen below 3 per cent, making our equivalent journey more difficult.

Second, once Portillo, Jones and Tebbit found work, they would feel well paid. In 2006 the average FTSE 100 chief executive earned 98 times more than the average UK worker; in 1979 that gap was just ten times.[6] And, as you might expect, this meant that the discrepancy between the wages of the young and the old was also far smaller. In 1974 the average 50–59-year-old earned 4 per cent more than the average 25–29-year-old; by 2008 that discrepancy was 35 per cent.[7]

Third, when they encountered problems at work, the unions, at least in theory, would protect their rights. In the late 1970s union membership included 50 per cent of the entire workforce. Today, it accounts for 29 per cent – the lowest in 60 years. These members are primarily in the public sector and the power of their organisations significantly diminished.

If these three features of our working life and theirs seem so different, there's a good reason: two completely contrary visions of how an economy should function were in play – one between 1945 and 1979, another between 1979 and the present day. The first resulted in a three-day week, numerous strikes, and several sterling crises ultimately requiring Britain to borrow money from the International Monetary Fund. The second saw greater national economic stability and fewer strikes, but occasional sterling crises and two big recessions – the latest of which has required Britain to nationalise the lion's share of its domestic banking sector. As all this would imply, both systems are flawed, but the prevailing consensus in our society is that the second system, under which we now live, works better than the first.

However, when examined from the narrow perspective of a young person starting work, our current economic system is obviously less successful, which is why 1.5 million of us are unemployed. That would never have happened in the post-war years for the simple reason that the consensus that existed in Britain until the 1970s saw full employment as the primary aim of government.

Following Britain's victory in the Second World War, successive Labour and Conservative administrations sought to rebuild the country. A Labour government led by Clement Attlee was elected on a promise to create what came to be known as 'the welfare state' and 'Jobs for All': 'We say, full employment in any case, and if we need to keep a firm public hand on industry in order to get jobs for all, very well', read Attlee's manifesto. 'No more dole queues, in order to let the Czars of Big Business remain kings in their own castles. The price of so-called "economic freedom" for the few is too high if it is bought at the cost of idleness and misery for millions.'

These ambitious words are starkly different from the mealy-mouthed offerings from Britain's modern political parties, but Britain was in an ambitious mood. The entire nation had already been galvanised to a single purpose – the defeat of Nazi Germany; and it seemed reasonable that it could show a similar unity during the ensuing peace. Pushed on by this momentum, Attlee's administration fundamentally remodelled the way Britain worked in just six years: establishing a tax-funded universal National Health Service, and giving legal structure to the idea that government should and could look after its citizens from cradle to grave and create thousands of jobs.

To do this, huge sections of the economy were brought under government control. This would be unthinkable now, but because Britain had just been through a world war in which huge swaths of its society had been centrally managed it was much easier. The Bank of England was brought under state control, as was almost all of Britain's major industry. Wage councils were established, and the price of goods, the movement of money in and out of the country, and high taxes were all fixed in accordance with the principles of two economists: William Beveridge, whose 1942 report into 'Social Insurance and Allied Services' fleshed out a vision of the modern welfare state; and John Maynard Keynes, whose 'General Theory' of economics stated that government must undertake active measures to ensure growth, investment and full employment. These were the basic ideas that informed government action for the next 30 years.

But there were consequences. Britain constantly felt that it was falling behind its European competitors. Too often the economy seemed to stop, head into recession and then surge ahead for a bit before slowing down again, the so-called 'stop-go' that made it difficult for businesses to thrive. Successive governments ended up fighting a guerrilla war with inflation as they sought to ensure growth and full employment. And that policy of low or no unemployment has a side-effect of driving wages up – since all workers are employed, they can demand the wages they want. Wages rose and, in order to cover costs, those selling and producing goods and services were forced to put up prices, leading to high inflation. That inflation then cancelled out the wage increase in the first place, creating a vicious upward spiral. There were other problems too. The value of sterling was fixed to the dollar after the war but by the late 1960s had to be devalued after foreign investors almost brought Britain to bankruptcy. By 1971 the pressures of inflation and international trade had combined to smash like a wrecking ball through Britain's post-war system.

In August 1971 the pound stopped being pegged to the dollar. And Britain's economy was left exposed when, two years later, oil prices more than tripled. Crippling fuel restrictions were imposed on the UK economy, and in 1974 the Heath government imposed a three-day working week, destroying businesses across the country. Strikes followed and never really stopped for the rest of the decade. Inflation spiralled out of control too, rising to 25 per cent, and under James Callaghan's Labour administration in 1976 the policy of full employment that had been the primary aim of post-war government became the secondary aim. By the end of the decade it would not be an aim at all. Margaret Thatcher won the 1979 election.

The Thatcher revolution

Margaret Thatcher has assumed an almost mythical status in recent British political history. In 2009 the *Sun* newspaper listed the '30 Ways Thatcher Made Britain Great', which included everything from her role in the fall of Soviet communism to the fact that she 'helped to perfect a way of preserving ice-creams as a chemist at J. Lyons & Co'.[8] She was the prime minister who stood up to Europe, defeated the Argentine navy and saved her country from IMF bail-outs, strikes and faltering economic growth. As she put it herself: 'We restored the strength and reputation of Britain.'[9]

It's a contention that seems difficult to argue with. For one thing, the 'stop-go' economics of the post-war period seemed to end under Thatcher. As Figure 15 shows, Britain's economy became definitively more stable after 1982.

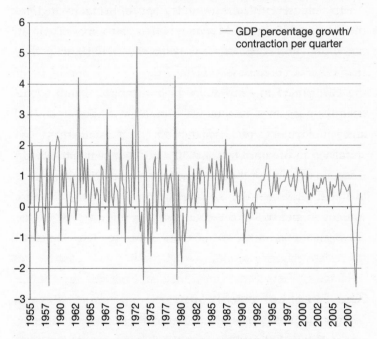

Figure 15. GDP percentage growth/contraction per quarter, 1955–2009 (Office for National Statistics).

Britain got much, much richer and the economy grew by 31 per cent under her stewardship – 10 per cent more than in the 1970s. And it all happened because, as Thatcher said herself, her objective was 'to turn round the whole philosophy of government'.[10] All of the fundamental elements of that postwar consensus were abandoned as soon as she gained office: privatisation placed the major industries back in the private sector; price controls, exchange controls, capital controls, were all abolished; she began the removal of wage councils and brought in strongly contested union regulation to ensure they could never hold the country to ransom again. In 1984 the National Union of Miners fought a year-long strike in an attempt to bring the nation to a halt and cow Thatcher as they had done her predecessors. They lost.

She aimed to allow individuals to create wealth – cutting the top rate of income tax from 80 to 40 per cent – and self-employment rose, evidence that entrepreneurship had returned to Britain. There was 'the big bang' when trading in the City of London enjoyed a renaissance and Britain became a world centre for the banking industry, which could move money in and out of the country freely and pay less tax on its dramatic earnings. All of these measures were designed to release Britain's economy from the iron grip of the state. Thatcher believed that individuals and not the government were best placed to decide the value of goods and services, shares and industries in the economy. As all this would imply, the policy of full employment, the primary aim of the postwar governments and their secondary aim after 1976, had been completely abandoned in favour of a less regulated free market, for which Britain required flexible labour.

The trouble is that, as you might expect, things aren't quite that simple. As Figure 15 shows, the first three years of the Thatcher revolution didn't produce any of the growth that her administration is given credit for. As a result of her policy of monetarism, which attempted to control the inflation that had frustrated the post-war governments by cutting government spending, the economy ground to a halt. It was a disaster. By 1982 joblessness had hit 3 million for the first time since the 1930s – there were 32 people chasing every job. Inflation itself didn't even fall, remaining in double figures and peaking in the summer of 1980 at 21.6 per cent – the highest since 1976.

Perhaps somewhere in the back of Margaret Thatcher's mind there was recognition that unemployment would be an inevitable and necessary feature of her reforms. One month into office, her government proposed its first significant piece of legislation – the biggest-ever rise in the social security budget, which would pay more money to the unemployed. But even this increase didn't do enough. As Thatcher unleashed 'market mechanisms', whole industries previously propped up in the post-war era were destroyed. Shipyards and mills were left abandoned, and in 1984, 20,000 miners were sacked at a stroke – provoking the strike. One *World In Action* documentary, 'On the Scrapheap', even recorded ranks of the mass unemployed of Birkenhead picking through rubbish tips for scraps that might augment their social security payments.

For all the bitterness that the reforms provoked, they proved so influential that the four prime ministers who have followed her have basically endorsed them. In this sense a new consensus, just like the agreement on basic principles between the parties in the post-war period, seems to have emerged.

After she left power, Mrs Thatcher was aiming for exactly this outcome, as she wrote in an article for *Newsweek* entitled 'Don't undo my work': 'Mr Major has accepted these principles, written them in his manifesto, held it up and said, "It's all me." What he means is that the things put in there were his choice. So I believe he will take that legacy forward.'

Under John Major, privatisation and deregulation continued; that Tony Blair and Gordon Brown accepted the new consensus has always caused confusion in some parts of the Labour party, but not only did they accept it, they were worthy inheritors of the Iron Lady's legacy. Both men recast Thatcher's free-market reforms as 'globalisation' – an unstoppable economic challenge that Britain must rise to. In 2005, 29 years after Callaghan was forced to concede that full employment was no longer his first duty, Blair set out how the rules of this new world work at the Labour party conference:

> I hear people say we have to stop and debate globalisation. You might as well debate whether autumn should follow summer. The character of this changing world is indifferent to tradition. Unforgiving of frailty. No respecter of past reputations. It has no custom and practice. It is replete with opportunities, but they only go to those swift to adapt, slow

to complain, open, willing and able to change. In the era of rapid globalisation, there is no mystery about what works: an open, liberal economy, prepared constantly to change to remain competitive. The temptation is to use Government to try to protect ourselves against the onslaught of globalisation by shutting it out. It doesn't work today. Our purpose is not to resist the force of globalisation but to prepare for it, and to garner its vast potential benefits. That's why education is Government's number one priority.

These are the features of the experiment in economics that began under Thatcher as 'neo-liberalism' and continued under Major, Blair, Brown and Cameron as 'globalisation'; and, as you can tell from Tony Blair's warning in the speech above, it's no longer simply a smart fix destined to ensure Britain's wealth and success, because other countries are now at it too. And that means that, with an economic system oiled by technological developments, businesses and workers across the world are in competition with each other. But what does all this mean for us?

Well, in the terms of this experiment we, the lab-rats, must adapt quickly, be highly skilled, and be prepared to 'constantly change', because an unforgiving force of impossible strength demands it. No longer will government help us by pulling the levers of the economy; instead it's down to us. For this reason, Tony Blair made a triple promise of 'education' to Britain before he was elected, determined that those entering the workforce would be better equipped for the global competition. In theory, we should all be well prepared to work in a 'globalised world'. Unfortunately, things turned out rather differently. So let's see what happens when our generation follow Norman Tebbit's example, jump on our bikes and pedal off into the globalised economy.

1. Buying our own education

Tony Blair said education was the first priority of his government because Britain's ability to compete in a 'globalised' world needs smart people to do clever stuff. And, if individuals are to be left to their own devices in that world, he figured it was probably important that they're equipped with a few skills to protect themselves. So even before they've taken Tebbit's bike out of the garage and pumped up the tyres, young people have been urged to get educated. And though the government has a poor record at keeping young people in education between the ages of 16 and 19 (drop-out rates are about 25 per cent, third-highest among developed nations),[11] the number of university places in Britain has expanded massively in the last twenty years. Today there are 1.5 million undergraduates in the UK, while in 1961 there were just 200,000. But this has meant some big changes. Those 1960s students received grants worth nearly £6,000 each year to live on while at university, and their fees were free. Since the competition for jobs is stronger now, and since education is the fundamental weapon of battle in the globalised economy, you might expect that the jilted generation would get these benefits too, perhaps even some more besides.

Instead we're getting less, much less. Not only do most English students have to pay for our own tuition – and these costs are among the most expensive in the world – but we get no grant, just a loan. In 2010, 335,000 students left university with an average of £17,500 of debt – that's before they've bought a house or got married, before they've even begun full-time work. And there's a more subtle problem with the way in which that debt is apportioned – it infantilises us. How much assistance the state will provide each student is contingent not on the wealth of the undergraduate, but on the wealth of their parents. And that's very odd. It's recognition by the state that school-leavers, despite the fact that they are legal adults, are still actually children formally dependent on their parents for their own lifestyles. As we will see, the government has other expectations for parents, whose wealth is too often called upon to subsidise low wages and internships, not to mention the high rents discussed in the previous chapter. The trouble is, as government continues to smooth the path for young adults to become reliant on their parents, it also undermines social mobility. Suddenly who your parents are becomes more important than ever.

And this effect might only increase under the new coalition government, since the costs of university education look set to grow. The coalition is pushing ahead with Labour's plans to sell off the student loans book to the private market for a profit (while it's debt for us, it's an asset for the government). Worse than that, the Liberal Democrats, who actually stood on a platform of abolishing student fees, may well permit the introduction of an even higher fee rate of £7,000 or the removal of the student fees cap altogether. Completing the break from past generations' university leavers, David Willetts, the new universities minister, described student funding as a 'burden on the taxpayer that had to be tackled'.[12] But it's unclear why this funding represents a burden today when it was a clear public benefit before 1998. And, actually, how great is that burden really? The total cost of student loans raised between 1998 and 2006 is just under £18.8 billion.[13] In national terms this is tiny, especially as it represents an average cost of £2.26bn a year – 2 per cent of the NHS budget. Even if the annual cost of loans rises to £5.5bn per annum over the next ten years,[14] as is predicted, that's still a remarkably cheap price to pay for equipping nearly half the population to face the awesome challenges of globalisation and grow the economy. Even so, perhaps Willetts has a point? Perhaps we shouldn't feel too bad about this, because we've been repeatedly told that graduates earn much, much more. In fact, we all know that, right?

Wrong. All the most serious data about graduate pay was obtained when there were far fewer graduates. So, in 1998, when Blair was seeking to justify the introduction of tuition fees, the government publicised a study which found that over a lifetime of work, graduates would be £400,000 better off than those with just two A-levels. The latest research estimates the advantage to be worth only around £140,000 for men and £160,000 for women. And, of course, the real value depends on what degree you do. Male graduates in maths and computing, for example, will gain over £220,000 in life-time earnings, while their peers in the English and History of Art departments will gain less than £25,000.[15] A recent survey by NatWest even suggested that some degrees will never make back their costs.[16] This isn't just unfair, it's a scandal. Simply by doing what the government has asked us to do, what we have been told is required in the global economy for our country to prosper, to build our own lives – even before thousands of young people have started on the journey to find work – they are saddled with debt.

2. The apprentice gap

Regardless of whether or not young people have a degree, they can't just walk into a job any more. Historically, one of the primary ways that they found work, particularly skilled work, was through apprenticeships whereby government subsidised on-the-job training for the new workforce. In the 1960s, for example, in the era when jobs were taken seriously, there were around a quarter of a million apprenticeships on offer each year. Today, with Britain's shaky economy – when work is harder to come by – there are 60,000 fewer. And while in 2009 the government announced that all qualified young people would have a right to an apprenticeship, 68 per cent of British companies haven't offered any; and even more – 85 per cent – didn't know that it was possible to receive government subsidies if they did so.[17] Even by its own standards, government isn't doing enough. All our politicians accept that Britain is in a globally competitive environment but they're failing to ensure that people get the skills to function in it.

3. Internships

The result is that many young people are forced to work as unpaid labour in a desperate attempt to get a foot on the ladder. Some describe this as a kind of soul-destroying quasi-enslavement, but in the globalised world there's another name for it: internship. It's a nice idea, of course, giving young people a few weeks' experience in their chosen field – but that's not how it really works. Internships can last for months at a time and are usually unpaid. This means that the young people who work for nothing at the start of their careers need wealthy parents to subsidise them. And, ultimately, for popular jobs in the media or the City, and many other jobs in London, this means the barrier to entry is money – you simply can't get them without experience, and you can't get the experience if you're from a poor background.

Eager to right this wrong, the last Labour government invented a half-baked 'Panel on Fair Access to the Professions' led by leading business people to come up with solutions. But far from getting on the side of young people, asking serious questions about why graduates are so ill-equipped to enter the workforce, or tackling the skills shortage, their report, published in the midst of the 2009 recession, showed just how little regard employers have for young workers. Their bizarre proposals included: that the number of internships on offer should be dramatically increased. They explained that internships are 'part and parcel of a modern, flexible economy and are useful both for interns and for employers. Where once they were an informal means of gaining practical insight into a particular career, today they are a rung on the ladder to success.'[18]

They also suggested 'a new national Kitemark for intern-ship schemes, recognising and rewarding best practice'; though they gave no detail of what this reward might look like, it would certainly not be a formal accreditation for interns themselves. They proposed, get this, 'changing the Student Loan system, so that interns can draw down their loan in four parts rather than three, to support summer vacation work', and the creation of 'micro-loans to cover short internships'.

You read that right. The government-appointed panel's suggestion for 'up-skilling' Britain's young people is to get the poorest to borrow even more money just to get into an office. And when they get there they will work for nothing because private businesses don't regard their contribution as mean-ingful enough to pay for. There are 1.5 million young people unemployed right now, and the best message the business leaders on that panel could send them is: if you want to work, borrow money you don't have so we can take your labour free of charge. What a shaming, condescending, ambition-crushing, contemptuous message that sends to a generation brought low by joblessness.

At least the panel drew a distinction between work experi-ence – designed to allow young people to discover if a career is right for them – and interning, where the idea is that young people actually work for businesses and begin to learn the ropes. But because there's no formality to internship, there can be no rhyme or reason to what the young people intern-ing actually do. Visit the website 'Interns Anonymous' if you want a flavour of how hard, repetitive and ultimately pointless many of the roles can be.

Case study: how to make money from internships

One man has worked out a way that might make money from internships. His name is Ben Rosen and he founded a website called inspiringinterns.com, for which he won BT's 'essence of the entrepreneur' award in 2009. Visitors to the site are greeted with a video of 'Harry the homeless man', a hypothetical story of a top Cambridge graduate who applied for dozens of jobs but, because he had no experience, was turned away and now lives on the street. Harry, explains inspiringinterns.com, should have got his act together and taken an internship.

It's a heavy-handed message, but the website seeks to attract graduates who are asked to submit their details and wait as inspiringinterns.com finds them full-time work placements. Perhaps that sounds brilliant, not least because the interns aren't charged for the service, but think again. While the interns' work is 'unpaid, but the company you'll work with will cover your travel and lunch expenses', as the website says, InspiringInterns charges fees to businesses to head-hunt interns for them. Once an intern is placed, InspiringInterns receives £500 for each month of work they do (for a minimum of three months), but none of that money is paid to the interns themselves. InspiringInterns tells businesses that interns can 'increase productivity' in a 'cost effective way', but this is a curious observation. If the interns themselves are really 'increasing productivity' – doing useful work – surely they deserve to be paid for it, and not Mr Rosen?

It's beyond doubt that interning, usually unpaid, is unofficially mandatory for those seeking employment in some professions,[19] particularly in the media, but it's impossible to say how many interns are currently photocopying, making tea, typing letters, writing articles, and buying food supplements for their bosses in Britain[20] – government measures only whether you're economically active. But studies suggest the numbers might be very high indeed. A report from the Institute of Employment in January 2010 found that, even four years after getting their degrees, 23 per cent of graduates in the creative sector were still undertaking unpaid work.[21] It's no surprise that the figures are so high. Quite apart from establishing the 2009 'Panel for Professionally Crushing the Dreams of Youth', in recent years the government has also activated 'Backing Young Britain,' an initiative aimed at 'uniting business and government to create thousands of opportunities for young people', which actually turns out to provide £40m of travel expenses for young people who must give their labour free. That's not Backing Young Britain into anything other than a corner. Meanwhile, the Department for Business, Innovation and Skills (BIS) recently launched its web-based Graduate Talent Pool, a scheme that matches employers with graduates but not, of course, for jobs. Instead they have really provided 5,000 internships.

This kind of unpaid work is probably not even legal. If you do meaningful work for a business, then, by law, you are entitled to the minimum wage.[22] But in 2009, Her Majesty's Revenue and Customs refused to prosecute a single complaint about internships. There isn't even a mechanism for recording how many interns complain of maltreatment. And actually plenty of interns are 'workers' doing real 'work',[23] but the government doesn't want to know.

When the Low Pay Commission investigated the issue, they were provided with 140 adverts for unpaid interns and work experience that appeared to break minimum wage rules.[24] But nothing will ever be done about this shameless injustice for two very good reasons: the interns themselves are so desperate for paid work that they have no motive for whistle-blowing; and regardless of what the Low Pay Commission says, government has a strong motive for promoting intern-ships – the rates of youth economic inactivity are disastrously high, and each young person who takes up an internship can come off the list at no cost to either government or employers. Simply put, young people are being encouraged to work for nothing to provide political cover for governments who have failed to equip them for work.

4. Unstable jobs

So what about the young people who actually make it and get a job? Once in the workplace the reality of being a member of a 'flexible workforce' begins to bite, because what 'flexible' really means is that workers are subject to the whims of the global marketplace and so, more often than not, they tend not to have stability. Job tenure – the amount of time people spend employed at the same organisation – has fallen by 20 per cent since 1975.[25] Crucially, the type of work that people undertake has become less permanent. The proportion of part-time jobs in the UK has risen by 5 per cent in the last two decades, and more men than ever, traditionally the least likely to be in part-time work, are filling these roles. Since 1984 the number of them in part-time jobs has increased from 630,000 to 1.8 million. This shouldn't be surprising. Of the 4.9 million new jobs created over the period, 2.6 million – more than half – are part-time.

As you might expect, it's young people who fill these part-time positions because they are usually easier to get than full-time ones. These are miserable conditions for any worker, but one study suggests that as many as one third of all first jobs are short-term contract jobs – which is remarkable when you consider that temping accounts for just 7 per cent of the jobs on offer.[26] But their work often isn't just part-time, it's also temporary. Apart from seasonal work, the main mechanism young people use to obtain temporary work is through agencies that take a cut of their wages in exchange for putting them in jobs. This is another obvious symptom of the new 'flexible' labour market, but if, unlike internship, agency work is paid at least, it's far from ideal. Nearly half of the people working in temporary jobs do so because they can find no other work. They have few employment rights, and when things go wrong there are numerous examples of both the agency, which takes a cut of their salary, and the company they are placed with, denying that they are the worker's employer. The work tends to exclude on-the-job training even when it's necessary, so there's a higher rate of workplace accidents. As the name suggests, the work is inherently insecure, and not only are conditions worse but temps also earn less.

On average, agency workers earn about 70p for every pound that a permanent worker earns for doing the same job.

Just as politicians have failed to protect interns, so EU legislation designed to improve the position of temporary workers has been fought by the UK government. When the TUC gave the government a lever-arch file of personal testimonies from unhappy temporary workers, as part of a decade-long campaign to get them these EU rights, government still gave in to pressure from businesses eager to keep temps cheap. So now the law says that temps must be in position for at least three months before they get employment rights – and, of course, because they are temporary, not many last this long. One estimate suggests that 65 per cent of all agency workers are under 35 years old.[27] This is a grim way to start a career, but millions of young people do it in order to find work. Young people will put up with a very great deal in order to get a foot on the ladder and begin their lives.

5. Poorly-paid jobs

In the previous chapter we showed that young people are buying less housing than ever before. What we didn't say is that when the Council of Mortgage Lenders decided to find out why this was, they noticed something very odd – 'a significant downward trend [in earnings] since the survey began in the early 1980s. The fall for the youngest age group is most significant, falling by six percentage points between the early 1990s and 2003. The 25–29 age group has made a small recovery but relative incomes still remain low historically speaking.'[28]

What the CML had discovered is what few people expect: even when most young people do get a foot on the career ladder and finally get the kind of proper job their parents walked into, they will almost certainly be earning proportionally less. If the UK economy is the room, this is the elephant defecating in the middle of it. Low pay, which is a formal measure of inequality,[29] is on the rise – 20 per cent of all jobs are low-paid in Britain today. In 1977, just 12 per cent were low-paid. And, inevitably, this rising income gap affects young people most dramatically, since they tend to start at the bottom. The average entry wage is now half the average national wage.[30]

Economists often talk about a 'rise in inequality' in Britain,[31] and there are arguments about how meaningful this inequality is. What few recognise is that inequality is not just a measure of rich and poor but, increasingly, a measure of the gap between young and old. And that's a problem for our generation because in the last decade Britain has become the most unequal society in the OECD – more than America, and more unequal than at any time since measurements began. Figure 16 shows what happened.

The younger you are in society, the less reward you get for your work. Over the last decade, the oldest members of the working population have enjoyed an increase in earnings of 40 per cent, while young people have got only 30 per cent. It appears that old people get the highest wage increases simply because they are older. And actually, if you take inflation into account you find that, for the youngest members of society, there's no meaningful wage increase – and all this during the greatest boom years of modern times.[32]

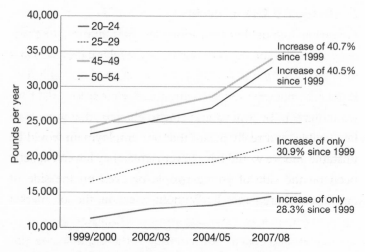

Figure 16. Median income by age group, 1999–2008
(HM Revenue and Customs, Survey of Incomes).

Some might say that this is just the nature of youth; that
young people are always poorer, that it's better to have tough
times earlier and enjoy the rewards later, but this isn't what's
happening here. The bottom line is that, as a result of low
wages and growing 'inequality', young people are much more
likely to be poor than at any time since the Second World War.
Even the OECD recognise this. In 'Growing Unequal', their
gargantuan 310-page study of inequality, they find that something very strange and extremely worrying has happened.
While people aged over 75 are less likely than ever to be poor,
'children and young adults have poverty rates that are now
around 25 per cent higher than the population average, while
they were below or close to that average 20 years ago'.[33]

It's not just that young people are more likely to be poor;
it's that in the past they were among the least likely.

Picking up the pieces

Politicians told us that education was their 'number one priority' and then forced us to pay for it ourselves; they said that
the benefits of the new global economy were 'vast' and then
watched while our relative earnings declined; they said we
would have to be 'willing and able to change', that we should
be 'flexible', but really meant that our employment would be
unstable and we would have fewer rights; they haven't exactly
been on the side of young people or even on the side of
employees more generally. Without question, the job market
for young people is a shambles, but you really get a sense of
the size of the political failure not from these simple descriptions but from the strategies that government has employed to
ameliorate the worst effects of this shambles. Labour pursued
three bold policies to tackle poor working prospects, policies
they claimed were a 'triumph'. They were the 'New Deal', the
minimum wage and the raising of benefits and tax credits. For
the young, all three have been a total failure.

When, in 2005, Tony Blair claimed that the Labour party's
'New Deal' for the unemployed had helped 1 million people
into work during a massive economic boom, he spoke as if he
was proud of what he'd achieved. In fact the New Deal has
been an expensive disaster, placing young people in temporary work or forcing them into pointless courses. Since 1997
it has cost Britain £75 billion.

No one satirised the Labour policy more aggressively
than the TV comedy *The League of Gentlemen*, which created
the character of Pauline Campbell-Jones, a sadistic careers
advisor with a fetish for biros who refers to her clients as 'dole

scum'. In one episode, in which Pauline attempts to get her clients to pretend to be *Big Issue* salesmen and beg for money as if homeless, she neatly sums up the circular bureaucracy around joblessness in modern Britain: 'You're nothing, you know that, you're worthless. Less than the shit on my shoe. I'm extending your restart by a month, then I'm sending you on a whole set of meaningless courses and then you're going to come back here and I'm going to re-restart you.'

Nearly 25 per cent of those placed on the 'New Deal for Young People' were retreads – constantly batted between temporary jobs and the retraining scheme – while two thirds failed to hold down employment for thirteen weeks or more. You can guess the result. Seventy-five billion quid later, there are now 1.5 million young people not in education, employment or training in Britain – more than when Blair took office.

But however grand Blair's boasts about the New Deal, there's another reform he's much more proud of. Wherever he goes, whatever he does, Tony Blair has a message about his time as prime minister of Britain, a key marker that tells us all why he's really quite brilliant and why the Tories aren't. He's the prime minister who brought Britain the minimum wage. He spoke about it in every Labour party conference speech he made after it became law. He mentioned it when he stood down, he even said it when he spoke to his former constituents in Sedgefield during his token endorsement of Gordon Brown's unsuccessful campaign for re-election in 2010: 'the changes that we delivered', he trilled, 'would never have happened under the Tories: and chief among them is a minimum wage.'

So what about this great claim to social justice? Well, it might have seemed like a good idea at the time, but in fact it doesn't work. For one thing, the way in which the minimum wage is organised makes absolutely no sense in Blair's flexible labour market. It's set by the government, but government can't react fast enough to changes in the wage market to keep it fair. So in 1999 it represented 47.6 per cent of average hourly earnings, two years later it had slipped to 45 per cent, but it was then raised and by 2007 it was up to 52 per cent. But if the minimum wage is poorly-administered, that's a sideshow compared to the fact that it's too low to live on.

In 2009 the Joseph Rowntree Foundation undertook research to discover how much money was required to have an acceptable standard of living in modern Britain. They concluded that a single person requires £13,900 a year, which is well above the minimum wage. Just to meet this criterion on the minimum wage, a person would have to work about 47 hours a week. But that's of course if you actually earn £5.73 an hour, and the truth is that young people don't. And that's deeply unfortunate because minimum wage jobs happen to be prevalent in the sectors where young people are most likely to work.

At the time of the report, for those under the age of 22, the minimum wage was £4.77 per hour; for those aged 16–17 the rate was £3.53. So now imagine that the single person in the Rowntree Foundation's investigation was aged 21. It would take them 56 hours a week to earn what's considered to be the most basic amount of money on which to subsist. That's equal to eight hours a day, every day of every week of the year. Just to make bare minimum. For those aged 17 it would be 75.7 hours a week.[34]

The minimum wage has affected the rest of the jobs market for young people too, because employers have used it as an excuse to introduce age-related pay in the private sector. After all, if the government thinks that young people should earn less, why shouldn't private companies agree? As the government's own Low Pay Commission concluded: 'Following the sharp rise in the NMW [national minimum wage] in October 2001, organisations in the fast food, pubs and restaurant sector began to introduce systems of age-related pay and now typically apply adult rates for employees aged 22 and over. McDonald's, KFC and Burger King have all introduced separate rates for younger workers over the last four to five years'.[35]

It's no surprise that the Commission also found that 'The relative position of young people aged 16–20 in the labour market has been worsening. Median pay levels have not increased at the same rate as those of older workers.' What's more, if entry wages are low, then investing in a university degree becomes a far more attractive option to all sorts of people who might, in other circumstances, prefer to be working. (For government to counter that influx into university by raising fees or cutting places really does leave young people with the worst of all worlds.)

So what, you might ask, has been done about the lack of a living wage? Well, the Commission recommended to the government that the minimum wage be raised for 16–17-year-olds by 7p, and by 9p for those under 22. Obviously this doesn't address the problem, but instead of tackling it they decided to commission some research and will report back in 2011. Which is a nice way of saying they've done nothing. Well, not nothing, they gave us 9p.

The minimum wage has failed so pathetically to shore up people's income that government has been left a single final refuge for ensuring that people have enough money: the benefits system that Margaret Thatcher was so keen to promote when she came to power all those years ago. Today, benefits are not only highly complex but also wildly costly. National expenditure on all of them, exclusive of pensions, is £89 billion, about one fifth of all government spending.[36] And there's a very obvious reason why the system costs so much: there are a great many people who are in work but don't earn enough, and a huge number who aren't in work at all and are supported – nearly one third of the UK population, 18 million in total.[37]

In order to help them fairly, however, government has created a mystifying total of 51 different benefits available to those with low or no incomes. They include benefits for families with young children, benefits for people on low incomes, benefits for the unemployed, the disabled and bereaved. In total, there are 8,700 pages of guidance from Whitehall to summarise how they're meant to work, and, unsurprisingly, this doesn't work very well. In short, the dozens of benefits that are available to people don't interact effectively with their actual lives, and this has a horrifying consequence: people who receive them are actually being discouraged from working.

The effect is so widespread now that there's even a name for it: 'the benefits trap'. What happens, for example, is that unemployed people find work and take jobs, but because, as we've seen, many more jobs than ever before are poorly-paid, their income doesn't match the money they were receiving while on the benefits that are taken away. How much they lose depends on what kind of person they are, but some find that as soon as they enter work, 90 per cent of their benefits are lost, making them just 10p better off for every pound they earn. So, a single person working sixteen hours a week on the minimum wage is only £8.63 a week better off than if they were unemployed, while a couple with two children and a private rent of £120 per week would be only £23 per week 'better off' if their earnings rose from £100 to £400 per week.[38] And none of these calculations take into account the cost of travel getting to and from work, or work clothes, or childcare, all of which could actually mean that by comparison to benefits, work makes you poorer. There are other preposterous features of the system too. It currently discriminates against couples who live together: 1.8 million would gain an average of £1,336 more in benefits if they lived apart.[39]

The new benefits model is completely different from 'the net, below which none can fall, but above which all may rise', as the saying goes. Instead we have a spider's web of bureaucracy from which those who land in it cannot escape. This is because government is trying to get the system to do much more than help up the very poorest in society: it's really attempting to use it as a mechanism of redistribution because pay is low and because there are so many people unemployed.

Case study: benefits discriminate against young people

In 2006 the government passed the Employment Equality Act, designed to end age discrimination in the workplace. In practice it protects ageing employees from getting the boot when they reach retirement age. And, somehow, state-sponsored age discrimination is still allowed as long as it's the young who suffer. Because employers are allowed to pay 16–17-year-olds £2.20 an hour less for their labour, this age group is effectively providing a £1.77 billion annual subsidy to businesses. It's a few billion more if you include 18–21-year-olds.

But it's not just in the field of minimum wage that the young are being discriminated against. Though they're statistically more likely to be poor, under-25s aren't entitled to working tax credit, a subsidy worth £6 billion and open to anyone else who's badly paid but happens to be older. Again, if you're unemployed and under 25 your jobseeker's allowance is worth 20 per cent less, simply on account of your age. You also lose if you try to claim housing benefit, because once again age matters. Single adults under the age of 25 are entitled only to a special category of benefit known as the 'Shared Room Rate', which, as the name implies, stops short of offering you your own room – they're just for real adults.

Meanwhile, at the other end of the spectrum, there's no end to the benefits. Over-60s receive benefits regardless of whether they need them or not: the winter fuel allowance worth £250 a year, a free TV licence for over-75s, the 'Christmas bonus' worth £10 ...

But the truth is that the system was never built to do this, so it's unsurprising that it doesn't work. In fact, when William Beveridge created his report setting the tone of the whole post-war consensus it never occurred to him that working people might not be able to afford the basics, because work paid enough to live on in the 1940s.

In fact, the first in-work benefits appeared 30 years later in a very significant year – 1976. The year is vitally important, since before that time it wasn't necessary to give in-work benefits, but afterwards it was. The benefits system was responding to a very particular change – 1976 was the first year when government decided that full employment was no longer the primary purpose of its policy. We all know that employment and benefits are related: the higher unemployment is, the more benefits must be paid by the state to unemployed people; but this isn't quite the case here – there's a more subtle link. What seems to happen is that when unemployment increases, benefits going to those people already in jobs have to increase too. That might seem pretty strange. After all, why should people in work need to be compensated if other people get laid off? It turns out that the relationship between unemployment and wages is at the beating heart of why benefits eat up so much of government spending, and why young people in Britain have such a terrible time in the jobs market.

How the job market really works

The labour market is just like any other market – the more labour supply there is, the cheaper labour becomes. As a result, unemployment creates a labour surplus that inevitably keeps wages low, which is why government started compensating people in jobs when, in 1976, unemployment began to rise dramatically. All that unemployment was affecting wages. If this labour surplus was a feature of Britain in the late 1970s, what about the 1980s – when full employment didn't just stop being the first objective of government, but stopped being any kind of objective at all? That policy of monetarism had driven unemployment to record highs of nearly 3.5 million people. So, what happened? Well, back in 1992 the documentary-maker Adam Curtis interviewed Sir Alan Budd, who was economic advisor to the Treasury during the first term of Thatcher's administration and was briefly head of the new coalition government's Office of Budgetary Responsibility in 2010.[40] This is what he had to say:

> I was involved in making … proposals which were partly adopted by the government … Now my worry is … that there may have been people making the actual policy decisions, or people behind them, or people behind them, who never believed that this was the correct way to bring down inflation. They did, however, see that this would be a very, very good way to raise unemployment … What was engineered there … recreated a reserve army of labour and has allowed the capitalist to make high profits ever since. I'm not saying I believe those stories but when I worry about all this, I worry whether that was really what was going on.[41]

Whether or not Thatcher's policy of monetarism created massive unemployment, and so a labour surplus on purpose, we don't know. What we know for sure, however, is that from the mid-1970s onwards it never, ever went away. Significant unemployment becomes a permanent characteristic of the UK economy, and, as a result, giving out benefits becomes an essential function of the UK government. (And with a labour surplus pushing down wages, getting off benefits becomes even less rewarding; the benefits 'trap' becomes harder to escape from.) The graph in Figure 17 lays it all

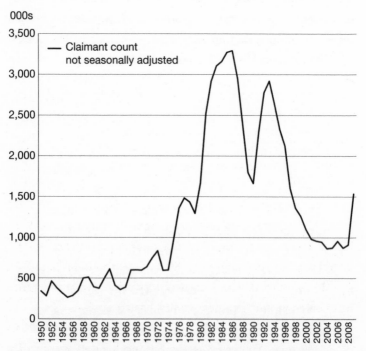

Figure 17. Recipients of unemployment benefits, 1950–2009 (Office for National Statistics).

out – it shows the number of people receiving unemployment benefits in Britain. During the post-war period, unemployment is low. As that consensus collapses the rate rises, and under Thatcher it explodes, never returning to much lower than 1 million people.

It was a paradigm shift. As you can see, between 1950 and the mid-1970s the terms of Britain's unemployment remain stable at between 300,000 and 600,000, but then the rate rises dramatically in line with recession and never again falls to these low numbers. But in reality things might be even worse than the figures suggest. As you can see from the graph, in the last fifteen years the rate of people receiving unemployment benefits has dropped considerably – still not to the lowest rates – but the non-working recipients of long-term sickness-related benefits have grown massively. In 1981, there were 570,000 claimants, today there are 2.7 million.[42] In towns like Easington in County Durham, one third of the entire population get it.

And there's another factor that creates a labour surplus: immigration. Where once Britain was a net exporter of people,[43] we're now net importers. At the end of 2009 there were 3.72 million non-UK-born people in employment in the UK, and that's a trend that has been continuing for years.[44] That is to be expected: in the last decade about half a million people came to Britain – mostly to work – every year. And from an economic perspective this has an obvious effect: just like unemployment, it adds to the labour surplus and drives down earnings. Young people in Britain bear the brunt of it too – between 2004 and 2006, 82 per cent of the 600,000 new migrants from the EU accession states were aged 18–35[45] and so are in direct competition with them for millions of jobs.

Whatever turns out to be the case, there's a connection between wages and labour, and if the connection was clear by the late 1970s (when Thatcher raised benefits), it has grown only more dramatic as a result of globalisation. Since companies can export jobs abroad at a moment's notice, capital is free to be truly international and, within the EU at least, so are workers. That means government can make no serious undertaking to poorly-paid employees any more. And all this leaves David Cameron, Nick Clegg and the rest of the gang in Westminster looking a little powerless. In a later chapter we'll examine exactly what effect their helplessness has on our politics, but you can get a sense of it from this excerpt from an interview conducted with Gordon Brown on *Newsnight* in the final weeks of the 2010 election campaign. Brown was being grilled by Jeremy Paxman, and was asked why he could do nothing about wages. His response was to squirm and grimace. He then said: 'Look, it's impossible, it's impossible in a global labour market to control the salaries of people, and it's not the right thing to do. See, I can't say that someone should be paid "X" in the United Kingdom, if someone can be paid "Y" for the same job in America or elsewhere.'[46]

He was angry. It was the anger of a man who knows his hands are chained, just as his predecessor Tony Blair suggested they would be in that conference speech about globalisation all those years ago. Brown knew he could no longer set wages any more than he could stop autumn following summer, as Blair might say. And he was obviously angry because he's perfectly aware of the human cost associated with this impotence.

He probably knows there's a further consequence of this labour surplus too. Between 1970 and 2000, the percentage of household income derived from wages dropped from 77 to 67 per cent.[47] The wealthy made up the gap in investments, the poor in benefits. It's a trend the OECD have started to kick up a fuss about since the recession began. They say the bargaining power of workers has been eroded and that 'workers may have had to make concessions on wages or working conditions to remain employed'.[48]

Now we begin to see what effect the globalised world is really having on employment. When Thatcher, Major, Blair and Brown point to the massive rise in GDP per capita that has occurred in the last 30 years, that there has been an explosion in wealth, they're committing a sinful omission. They're not admitting what has really happened to people's wages. For that you need to see the graph in Figure 18. It shows that the real winners in the new consensus are not hard-working British families – their share of Britain's annual income actually declined by about 10 per cent. No, the winners are Britain's private corporations and their owners, whose income has increased by the same amount.

So where does all this leave us? Well, put simply, it leaves young workers in Britain poorly-paid or jobless, unstable and fearful, because a surplus labour market also tends to make jobs more unstable. After all, what's the point of giving people rights in work if there are a dozen around the corner to replace them at any given moment? As we've seen, a vast

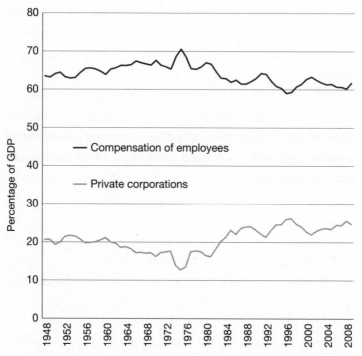

Figure 18. Where the money went: make-up of GDP over time, 1948–2008 (Office for National Statistics).

swath of young people start their lives in casual or fixed-term work and plenty continue in the same vein. And, it turns out, a casual worker is three times more likely to become unemployed and a fixed-term contract worker is 2.5 times more likely to become unemployed than a permanent worker.[49] Young people are yo-yoing in and out of the jobs market, swapping benefits for low-paid jobs all the time.

And the result of all this is that people are scared. They're scared of being poor, and scared of losing their jobs once they've finally got them. That's even better for corporate profits because scared workers don't ask for more rights and don't ask for more stability and don't ever, ever ask for more money. What's more, the smarter of the rich old men running the global economy have known this all along. Back in 1995, Alan Greenspan, the former chairman of the US Federal Reserve and perhaps the single most important man in international economics, admitted what most of us have taken years to discover:

> Overall job growth has remained substantial but that seems not to have relieved the fear of displacement. And that fear has doubtless played a significant role in the slowdown in growth of labour compensation as workers have in effect sought to preserve their jobs by accepting lesser increases in wages. While disciplined monetary policy is largely responsible for the disinflationary trends of the last 15 years, subdued wage pressures have doubtless facilitated those trends. There eventually will come a point, however, when workers will perceive that it no longer makes sense to trade off wage progress for incremental gains in expected job security. The concern about job loss will not have diminished, but there is a limit to how far it can go.[50]

So, how far can all this really go? We begin to get the shape of
the answers in Blackburn as that funeral cortège drives to the
old Masonic Hall carrying the body of a determined girl who
applied for 200 jobs and got turned down for every single one.
Rejections of this kind take their toll on a person, but actually
it's not rejection that most young people find so traumatic.
Employment means something deeper. Even if the global
economy commodifies labour into wages and hours worked,
that's not how most of us see it. Employment gives us dignity and responsibility, possibility and opportunity. Without
it, young people can't begin to find meaning, find purpose,
find our place. And this will be our generation's tragedy, told
through 100,000 statistics each casting new light on a million
individual struggles and all pointing to one simple, irreduc-
ible, obvious conclusion: that we weren't allowed to grow up
with time enough to live our lives.

The statistics are already being compiled. We now know
that poorly-paid unstable jobs make people less likely to
co-habit, less likely to marry, less likely to reproduce, that
'when the labour market position of men is characterized by
instability, then this is at least partially transferred to their
family life'.[51]

And nothing's more likely to undermine Britain's labour-
surplus economy than too few new workers. Of course, we
will have children, we will get married, but just as we don't
get a decent wage until we're older – just as we have to intern
and temp – everything is delayed for us; and with this delay,
so the narrative of our lives begins to crumble. For 'how can
long-term purposes be pursued in a short-term society? How

can durable social relations be sustained? How can a human being develop a narrative of identity and life history in a society composed of episodes and fragments?' How can we, when 'the conditions of the new economy feed on experience which drifts in time, from place to place, from job to job'?[52]

This is our story. We're in the closing moments of that grand experiment played out on us by predecessors who started their work before we were ever born, who abolished the stop-go economy and gave us stop-go lives, who gave us a knowledge economy and then charged us for the knowledge, who removed all stability and wonder why we stumble. And in this grand experiment we can already guess the conclusion. It's run long enough for the predictions to flow. In the OECD, the very citadel of international economic co-operation in the globalised world, they're already filing the papers: 'Growing inequality is divisive', says OECD secretary-general Angel Gurría. 'It polarises societies and divides regions within countries. It carves up the world between rich and poor, stifles upward mobility between generations. And talented and hard-working people don't get the rewards they deserve.'[53]

Infantilised. Marginalised. Ultimately stigmatised. We did not, and do not, and will not get what we deserve. But this story isn't done yet. It will end as it began, with the 'undeserving poor', that recurring, tragic feature of our history about which rich old men can say so much and know so little. Today, in the minds of those men, the undeserving now number 1.5 million who are young, and millions more besides. These are the people who, in the grand narrative of labour-surplus capitalism, have come to represent the surplus and not the labour, to whom we offer up pity and anger in turns, money and incredulity in turns, to whom we give so very, very much and yet so little. Right here, in the spinning core of this time-honoured but wholly dishonourable argument, sits profound absurdity. What we know for sure is that before Thatcher's economic 'miracle', when full employment was the first priority of government, the undeserving poor didn't really exist – there were enough jobs, and those jobs were worthy of their workers. And yet those men who championed her reforms, who nurtured their success, and who celebrated as free-market capitalism spread throughout the world as consensus, are also the same men who stigmatise the undeserving poor, who told them to get on their bike, who considered removing their support entirely, who asked them to starve. What irony it is that the very economic revolution they supported actually created the idle people they now so despise.

It shouldn't be possible for those men to ignore any more the link between huge welfare payments paid to the unemployed, and a job market dominated by a labour surplus with poorly-paid and insecure jobs. It's true, Britain can no more go back to the economics of the 1970s than it can restore the workhouse to its towns and cities. Time has moved on. But if swaths of unemployed young people remain stuck on benefits in 2070, we will have failed. Blair was correct when he made the triple promise of 'education' for Britain: only highly skilled workers can flourish in the new century. But he broke that promise too. Britain continues to fail to equip people for the challenges of the global market, and we know this because even the best-educated are now forced to work for nothing when they thought they would be earning. We know this because it's a battle to get an apprenticeship, a bare-knuckle fight to pay down the cost of a degree, and something close to a miracle if your New Deal training ends in a permanent position with prospects, rights and benefits. For 30 years we haven't done enough to safeguard the prospects of our workers. The consequences are written in millions of pages of benefits applications, on the faces of our generation, on the margins of our society. Enough now.

INHERITANCE

3

INHERITANCE

'In this world nothing can be said to be certain, except death and taxes.'

Benjamin Franklin, letter to Jean-Baptiste
Leroy, 13 November 1789

'Now well over a third of home-owners in Britain have the threat of inheritance tax hanging over them. These are people who have worked all their lives. People who have saved money all their lives. People who have already paid taxes once on their income. People whose only crime in the eyes of the taxman is that instead of spending their savings on themselves, they want to pass something on to their families. People who feel the most basic human instinct of all: they aspire to a better life for their children and their grandchildren. Our Government will be on their side.'

George Osborne, speech to the Conservative
party conference, 1 October 2007

If nothing can be certain except death and taxes, it's when taxes are raised at the point of death that people get really pissed off. Poll after poll finds that inheritance tax is the most unpopular of all Britain's taxes, and it has been for years.[1] And this is remarkable because, unlike VAT for example, not everyone pays it – those same polls regularly find that at least one third of the population don't expect to receive any inheritance at all. So what explains this?

People consistently say it's unfair. You can see their point. The giving of our wealth at death to those who come after us entrusts what remains of our worldly future in them, so the idea of taxing that seems to break that 'most basic human instinct of all': the aspiration 'to a better life for their children and their grandchildren', as Britain's chancellor has said. His 2007 speech on the subject was a great success.[2] Tapping into the visceral emotion of the British electorate, it transformed the Conservative party's standing in the polls and persuaded Gordon Brown, who had just months earlier been selected by the Labour party to serve as prime minister, to call a halt to his general election plans. Since then, the Conservative pledge to raise the inheritance tax threshold to £1 million has remained one of the party's most popular policies, though in the current climate of austerity they might not implement it any time soon. But this chapter isn't about inheritance tax.

Though most people seem to believe that personal inheritance is the main mechanism by which future generations gain wealth, this isn't necessarily the case in modern Britain. There's another type of inheritance that leaves a far broader legacy than whatever people can personally hand down as individuals. This second type of inheritance doesn't lend itself to headline-grabbing policy-making, but it will affect us all – whether or not we inherit from our parents in the decades that follow. It's our national inheritance: the buildings and institutions created and enhanced by those who come before us, the investments those generations make, and the debts they build up through government and private institutions. It's the big picture of what generations pass on from one to another, but for the jilted generation this picture is pretty grim.

We've already seen one corner of it: massive national debt. Bailing out the banks, propping up the car industry, and a temporary cut in VAT were all measures undertaken in an attempt to revive a failing economy in the midst of the worst global financial crisis since the Great Depression – and all of them cost Britain money. At the same time, the expense of just doing what government had been doing already still had to be met at a time when tax revenue was falling. Some governments cut back, but when things went wrong, the Labour administration in charge argued that if they pulled the plug on the public sector there would be more job losses and the recession would get worse. So to fix the problem they decided not to put up taxes, but to borrow against the country's collective mortgage, the UK's national debt. Now it's payback time.

Actually, from the perspective of the jilted generation, it's payback time for the rest of time. Because, in order to continue to pay for the running of all government departments, schools, hospitals, councils, as well as paying public-sector pensions and state pensions and all the other stuff government coughs up for, Britain has built up an overdraft of £890 billion.[3] Like any loan, there's a charge for borrowing the money. In 2011, we'll have to pay 3.5 per cent of our GDP just to service that interest on the debt – around £48 billion in cash terms.[4] And guess when we'll finally pay it off: 2046[5] – the year when the very oldest members of the jilted generation start to retire.

But here's a funny thing: nobody is talking honestly about where this burden will fall. One of the most absurd spectacles of the 2010 election campaign was watching the Labour and Conservative parties attempt to bolster their ideas by press-ganging dozens of hapless economists onto the letters pages of newspapers; some urging government not to cut public expenditure but raise business taxes, others pushing aggressively for more dramatic cuts in spending to help pay down the debt more quickly. Phalanx after phalanx of academics, business leaders and VIPs were roped in by both sides as living proof that only their policies could get Britain 'back on its feet' or 'safeguard our future' (insert your own hackneyed slogan here). But in all this earnest debate about being 'responsible', as Clegg, Cameron and Brown all claimed to be, no one actually seemed to stop and point out the obvious: that the people whose opinions really matter on the subject of Britain's national debt are the jilted generation. We're the ones who will end up paying it off.

The election was the ideal time to engage the nation in a serious discussion about what we want from government and what we're prepared to pay for. For reasons we'll discuss in the next chapter, this didn't happen. And things get stranger still because, contrary to what politicians of all persuasions like to pretend, Britain's true debt is much greater, much more deeply ingrained into our system of government, and much more likely to damage the prospects of Britain's new adults than many politicians admit.

Pensions: the debt that keeps on growing

If you know that Britain is in debt you probably also know that we have a 'pension crisis' and that an argument of some kind has been rumbling on about it for years. The trouble is that it's not entirely clear exactly what the point of disagreement is. Charities like Age UK believe the 'crisis' is 'pensioner poverty that blights the lives of millions'.[6] Others, like Joan Bakewell, a retired broadcaster who was very briefly Labour's 'champion for the elderly', feel the crisis is that older people have been marginalised: 'I receive a steady stream of letters from older people', she explained in one government press release, 'providing clear evidence that they feel marginalised and undervalued.'[7] But there's another crisis too: never mind marginal increases on pensions, how exactly are we going to pay for them at all?

Since the recession began, private pensions in the UK have taken a battering. Our private pension schemes are now looking at a shortfall of £200bn – nearly six times more than when recession hit – and this problem has been dramatically exacerbated by the pension stealth tax created by Gordon Brown, which has removed at least £100bn from the value of these funds. And, as the economy has only slowly begun to recover, this tax just makes it more difficult for the pension firms to make up the shortfall.[8] But if the funding of our private pensions is in a bad way, public pensions are much worse. Since 2004, the annual state pension payments made by government to British citizens have skyrocketed by a third to a little less than £80 billion. These payments now account for 12 per cent of total government spending,[9] and the expense is set to grow dramatically because Britain's demographics are shifting.

In 1971, people aged under 30 made up nearly half the population; now they make up barely one third. And while the proportion and absolute number of young people has declined, we now have more pensioners. In 1971, over-60s made up one in five of the population. By the time the last of the baby boomers retire in 2030 they will make up almost one in three. Figure 19 shows what is predicted to happen.

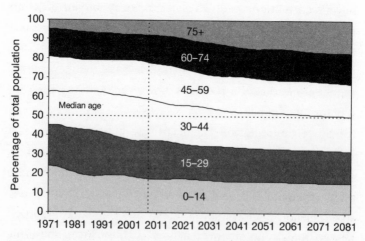

Figure 19. Percentage age distribution, UK, 1971–2083
(2008-based National Population Projections, Office for National Statistics, 21 October 2009).

Not only will there be more pensioners and a higher pension bill, there will also be fewer people – that's us – to help pay for it. So far, not a single thing has been done to remedy the situation. It took government years to realise there was even a problem. Professor Martin Weale of the National Institute of Economic and Social Research explains: 'The rise [in old-age life expectancy] was so sudden and unexpected that the statisticians thought it was a blip and the trend would return to normal. But it didn't. By the 1990s it was known that people were going to be living for much longer but nothing was done about it.'[10]

You might think that by 2010 it would be quite straightforward to lessen this burden on the shoulders of Britain's young people. After all, if there's a pension pot out there, we could make it 'work harder', either by investing it into new businesses or by using it to help to pay down some of our national debt. And when the fortunes of Britain's economy pick up, the problem might be solved, right?

Wrong. There is no pension pot. Instead, the British government has always operated a pay-as-you-go state pension scheme. The theory is that every worker in Britain pays into it through National Insurance and this cash is then immediately distributed to the current crop of pensioners. Workers don't pay for their own retirement; they foot the bill for those people who are in retirement already. In this respect the UK state pension operates like a 'Ponzi scheme' – almost identical to the operation run by the New York investor Bernie Madoff. The only difference is that no one is lying about how pensions work. Both systems work on the basis that there's always more money being paid in than out. But as soon as that balance tips over, the system is left exposed. Because of this high risk, Ponzi schemes are completely illegal, and when Madoff's crooked venture was uncovered, he ended up in a US Federal Prison. But the only people who will be punished for the failure to take tough decisions on pensions will be us.

What should have happened is that all pay-as-you-go schemes should have been readjusted a long time ago; every worker should have been paying in for what they would receive later in their (greatly extended) retirement. In other words, our parents should have saved much, much more. One option would have been for government to have saved much more money by raising National Insurance contributions to fund the shortfall, another would have been for private individuals to have prepared better for their retirement so government intervention wasn't necessary – but, since no one admitted the situation, this didn't happen. And the long-term costs of short-term thinking have built up. The Government Actuarial Department[11] estimates that the unfunded part of UK pension liabilities now equals £2.2 trillion. Of this figure, £1.4 trillion will pay state pensions and £800 billion will pay comparatively generous pensions to public-sector employees. Regardless of what's done around the fringes, the hard fact is that Britain's young people will bankroll the entire scheme. That means our pay packets will be smaller than they otherwise would have been, and the costs of living our own lives, raising kids and providing for the next generation will be harder to afford.

Just as Britain's burgeoning pension crisis has roots that stretch back decades to the baby boom, so too does the forthcoming crisis in healthcare. When people live longer they don't just need a larger pension, they also need more medical treatment.

One of the basic advantages of being young is that, when you ignore the odd indulgent mother shoving junk food through the railings surrounding schools that serve Jamie Oliver-style school dinners,[12] we are healthy. That means we're very cheap customers for the National Health Service. The average annual spending per head on those aged between 16 and 44 is just £350; the cost of treating people who have retired is £2,700. Almost half of the entire NHS budget is currently spent on pensioners.[13] The reason why they're so expensive is that Britain's elderly are not just living longer, but living longer as sick people. In the last twenty years, there has been a 25 per cent increase in the amount of time people live as permanently unwell at the end of their lives,[14] and the trend should continue. All this means that, while in 1990 the cost of the NHS was 5 per cent of Britain's entire GDP, by 2040 the Treasury expects that cost to rise to 10 per cent[15] – and, once again, these are costs that our generation must pay.

Britain's hidden debts

There are other aspects of Britain's inheritance that are much more sinister: parts of our debt that were hidden in balance sheets by those who knew that they were borrowing from future generations. By far the most egregious example is the Private Finance Initiative (PFI) – a system specifically

designed to ensure that the cost of current government investment projects will be heaped onto the shoulders of future
taxpayers.

This is how it works. Traditionally, if the government
wanted to build a school or a hospital, it would take a chunk
of taxpayers' money and build it. The difficulty in doing this
is that it's hard to raise lump sums of money all in one go. If
the government borrows cash to spread the cost, it's obliged
to place that debt on its balance sheet. This comes with a
downside. When public debt grows, the money markets and
political opposition accuse the government of being irresponsible.[16] Also, in the last three decades, governments drawn
from all three main political parties have been convinced that
the public sector isn't as good as the private sector at manag-
ing these projects, and so have been reluctant to undertake
them. These are all big problems to which the Major government hit upon a cunning solution in the early 1990s: why not
ask the private sector to build your new hospital for a long-
term annual fee?

That sounds good – a bit like a mortgage. Unfortunately
it's more like renting. For one thing, government doesn't have
to pay for the costs of upkeep on the item bought through
PFI; for another, it never owns the property that it's paying
for. PFI contracts are very long-term, though, which tends to
lock government into paying fees for facilities that may seem
vital now but are less necessary in the future. As one MP
concluded in 1996, when the Major government was getting
stuck in to PFI: 'apparent savings now could be countered by

the formidable commitment on revenue expenditure in years to come.'[17]

Now here's a funny thing. The man who said that was the last Labour chancellor of the exchequer, Alistair Darling. And, far from shying away from PFI schemes, they became critical to Labour's management of the economy between 1997 and 2010. The total value of all the local and central government PFI projects under Labour is estimated to be a whopping £56bn. PFI was an ideal way for New Labour to invest in its first term when it had committed to 'stick to Tory spending plans' but wanted to be seen to do more than them. As Alan Milburn, then a junior minister in the Department of Health, admitted two months after Labour took office: 'when there is a limited amount of public-sector capital available, as there is, it's PFI or bust.'[18]

Today the situation looks much more like 'PFI and bust', because PFI shares a final characteristic with renting: it's much more expensive than buying outright. While the total 'capital value' of Labour's PFI schemes is £56bn, they will cost Britain just a tiny bit more: £267 billion[19] – 60 per cent of which will be spent on servicing the debt – which begins to look like very bad value for money indeed. Worse, £214.5 billion is due after 2011.[20]

PFI is a bad deal in other ways too. Take Milburn's own former department, the NHS, which represents 20 per cent of PFI spending. When Britain's debt to the private companies that built hospitals and surgeries on our behalf is finally paid back, we'll have infrastructure worth £11.2bn but we'll have paid £63bn. Right now we still owe £56.7bn for Labour's healthcare projects, and we'll finally pay it off in 2046 when the buildings will be 50 years old – right around the time that members of our generation will want to use them.

PFI has been used all across Britain to build schools, roads, courthouses and computer systems. Even the UK Treasury building itself was redecorated using a PFI scheme that will take 35 years to pay off. This final scheme was a 'success' – in that it doesn't represent tear-your-hair-out bad value for money – but many are disastrous. The Parliamentary Public Accounts Committee reports into PFI are now legendary for their condemnation of financial incompetence.[21] In truth, the PFI bill is the true cost of sheer political cowardice. Neither the Labour nor the Major governments were prepared to really pay for the investment they wanted to make, so they took the credit instead and now today's young people will foot the bill. That's a poisonous inheritance for any generation to pass on to their children.

What the bill might look like

You've probably already noticed that the sums of money required to pay down the debt, to pay for pensions and health-care and PFI, are starting to mount up – but now it's time for the really bad news: let's add it together. During the height of the recession in 2009, when a team of European economists based in Munich decided to do an audit[22] of Britain's long-term finances, they discovered something extremely unsettling happening in Britain: most of our liabilities – the money we owe – is 'implicit'. Like PFI, these liabilities don't show up on the government's balance sheet. And, in their opinion, the total value of that debt is equal to 510 per cent of GDP – twice as much as France and Germany, more even than the USA.[23] They concluded: 'The UK is at the very bottom of our sustainability ranking ... living their current public life on credit while Continental Europe has at least achieved some fiscal responsibility.'[24] Worse, in the interests of statistical rigour and fair comparison, they decided to use pre-recession figures from a 'good year'. Their conclusions were drawn from data in 2004, before we suffered a massive recession, before we paid for the bail-out of several banks, before we incurred the biggest deficit in our history. The total now is much, much worse, and the consequences will be profound not just in terms of high taxes and poor public services but for another, hidden, reason.

Back at the National Institute for Economic and Social Research, Professor Weale says that in strict economic terms there's 'a shadow cost' to all this debt. When Britain has to pay back money, government takes taxes from your income and as a result stops that money going back into the productive part of the economy. So when the debt equals 60 per cent of GDP, it depresses the nation's stock of income-producing assets by about 30 per cent,[25] so it's actually harder to pay the money back than you might expect.

This isn't a simple numbers story. These implicit debts, already written into the ledgers of thousands of pages of local and central government departmental budgets, represent something more – they are workers impoverished by higher taxes and lower living standards, they are life chances not taken and businesses held back. For us, the jilted generation, they represent the price we will pay merely for being born. Is this fair?

We've discussed a good number of issues in this book that we think heap an unfair burden upon our generation, but this doesn't merely represent an unfortunate situation – it's plain injustice, for three good reasons: debts that the jilted generation must pay have been built up as a result of imprudent management of the economy; chunks of our common inheritance have been sold off; and the money spent and advantages enjoyed by previous generations are not available to us.

To take the first point, it seems reasonable that if you raise a debt for yourself, you shouldn't force those who live on long after you die to pay it off. This isn't a new idea. Thomas Jefferson, a principal author of the US Declaration of Independence and fourth president of America, wrestled with the problem of debts across generations and came to a pretty firm conclusion. 'I sincerely believe ... that the principle of spending money to be paid by posterity under the name of funding is but swindling futurity on a large scale.'[26]

Jefferson argued that no generation had a right to absolute possession over the earth. Each generation, he believed, was merely a 'tenant for life'. And, if they raised debts to be paid by the next generation, they would no longer be a tenant in life, but a tenant in death as well. In other words, passing on the burden of debt was a form of extortion from beyond the grave. Jefferson found this thought to be abhorrent, and declared: 'The earth belongs always to the living generation.'

Jefferson felt so strongly about this that he even lobbied his fellow founding father, James Madison, to have this principle written into law, because he believed that no one, not even the government, had the right to burden the next generation. 'Neither the representatives of a nation, nor the whole nation itself assembled', he wrote, 'can validly engage debts beyond what they may pay in their own time.'[27] Of course, there are circumstances in which the raising of debt for future generations to pay might seem reasonable. For one thing, most people expect societies to get richer over time, so it's easier for those in the future to pay for debt than it is for those who live now – though there's no guarantee of this, of course. Further, there are circumstances, like the global financial crisis or world war, that present threats to the continued success of a society. In these circumstances, doing what it takes to ensure survival and to ameliorate a catastrophic failure in society is reasonable. However, these particular circumstances justify only a fraction of Britain's current debt – they certainly don't explain PFI or the pension crisis, or any of the 'fiscal irresponsibility' described by those Munich economists that occurred before the global recession.

Second, since all generations have a claim to common property owned by the government or the nation, no single generation can exploit that property solely for their own ends, and to the exclusion of everyone else to come. In the name of intergenerational justice, a number of legislatures around the world have tried to embody this principle in their constitutions, notably in environmental terms. For example, in 1971 voters amended the Pennsylvanian constitution to read: 'The people have a right to clean air, pure water, and to the preservation of the natural, scenic, historic and esthetic values of the environment. Pennsylvania's public natural resources are the common property of all the people, including generations yet to come. As trustee of these resources, the Commonwealth shall conserve and maintain them for the benefit of all the people.'[28] Similarly, the Norwegian constitution was redrafted in 1992 to declare that: 'Natural resources should be managed on the basis of comprehensive long-term considerations whereby this right will be safeguarded for future generations as well.'[29]

We don't discuss the environment in this book, but a glance at something like fish stocks would suggest that this aspect of our common inheritance has been exploited ruthlessly and to the exclusion of all other generations.[30] However, we believe that a similar principle applies well beyond these or other environmental issues. Take the mismanagement of public housing. As we've already seen, millions of council houses were sold during the 1980s. There's nothing wrong with selling common property per se, but what happened under 'right to buy' was unjust because the benefits of that sale were enjoyed by just one generation. Just one generation were able to buy the houses cheaply, and when government received money from them, it tended not to reinvest it for future generations but effectively spent it in the form of tax breaks. As a result, this fire sale will never happen again, few public homes have been built subsequently, and Britain is left with council housing lists that stretch for decades. In this way, one generation took advantage of another. As we'll see further on in this chapter, the same has happened with other elements of common property like North Sea oil and the nationalised industries. But why is it unfair for one generation to sell that which is held in common? The answer is pretty simple. If something isn't yours to sell, then appropriating it represents a form of theft.

This brings us to the third reason: the failure of reciprocity. This is the idea that if you receive something, you have an obligation or duty to pass it on in turn. And a good example of how this principle has broken down is in universities. None of the Tory and Labour ministers involved in scrapping grants and introducing tuition fees or top-up fees ever had to pay a penny to go to university. They were paid to do so. Their parents' generation gave them this benefit because tertiary education was thought to be a public good; something that the whole of society would benefit from. For these ministers to levy a charge on the next generation of students represents a blatant failure to reciprocate.

Many of the other injustices that we talk about in this book also fall into this category: the scrapping of mortgage interest tax relief, the ending of the promise of full employment, the changes in tenancy rights, the lack of a public house-building programme. And as we'll see below, there are other issues like a failure of investment that add to the indictment. And the egregious and damaging result is the denial of the terms of adulthood. As we've seen, an entire generation's ability to start families and have children has been made more difficult because our parents are failing to pass on the benefits they received from the generation before them. But why are generations obliged to pass on benefits received from their parents? Some would say that every generation is free to do exactly what they want – what's so unfair?

The answer to this question was articulated by Edmund Burke – an English philosopher and contemporary of Jefferson – in a concept he called the 'eternal society'. Reflecting on the revolution that had just taken place in France in 1789, Burke wrote that: 'Society is indeed a contract. Subordinate contracts for objects of mere occasional interest may be dissolved at pleasure – but the State ought not to be considered nothing better than a partnership agreement in a trade of pepper and coffee, calico or tobacco, or some other such low concern, to be taken up for a little temporary interest, and to be dissolved by the fancy of the parties.

'It is to be looked on with other reverence; because it is not a partnership in things subservient only to the gross animal existence of a temporary and perishable nature. It is a partnership in all science; a partnership in all art; a partnership in every virtue, and in all perfection. As the ends of such a partnership cannot be obtained in many generations [by themselves], it becomes a partnership not only between those who are living, but between those who are living, those who are dead, and those who are to be born.'

So if a generation accepts its role in that partnership, and the benefits that come with it, not just in economic terms but also in terms of those wider societal bequests like culture, art, science and literature, then each generation has a duty and an obligation to maintain that link in turn. Burke also argued that the very purpose of government was to maintain that common inheritance: 'One of the first and most leading principles on which the commonwealth and the laws are consecrated is … that they ['the temporary possessors and life-renters'] should not think it amongst their rights to cut off the entail or commit waste on the inheritance by destroying at their pleasure the whole original fabric of their society; hazarding to leave to those who come after them a ruin instead of a habitation.'

Extortion, theft, evasion of contracts; it sounds like a rap sheet for Britain's most wanted. But do the charges stack up? One way to find out is to compare the behaviour of previous generations. Examine, for example, our parents' parents, that 'greatest generation' who won the most horrific war the world has ever known, who established a national system of healthcare and free education, and built millions of homes for their children to live in. All of this is remarkable, but what is equally significant is that they did this while paying off huge war debts.

How previous generations acted

In reality, most of this money wasn't to pay for the cost of war itself but to pay for the aftermath. After VE Day, Britain took out a £586bn loan to help begin the reconstruction of the country. Paid over a 35-year period, that generation successfully reduced the war debt from 250 per cent to 52 per cent of GDP by 1976, when the oldest baby boomers turned 30.

Now compare this to what happened when younger generations came of age. During the mid-1970s something strange happened: national debt wasn't reduced any further. Although the percentage owed remained the same, the

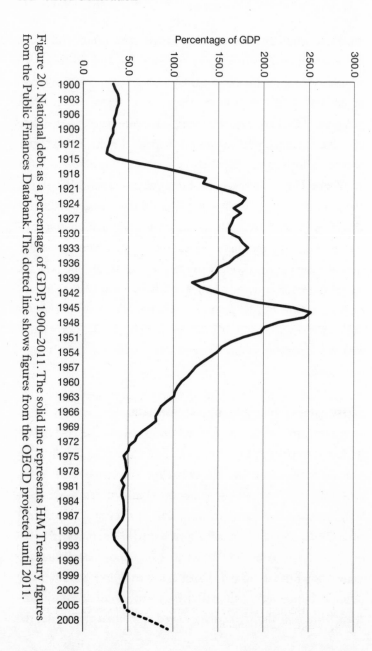

Figure 20. National debt as a percentage of GDP, 1900–2011. The solid line represents HM Treasury figures from the Public Finances Databank. The dotted line shows figures from the OECD projected until 2011.

absolute amount increased dramatically as total GDP rose. It's the equivalent of extending your mortgage after your house price goes up. And between 1970 and 2004 the debt remained at 46 per cent as the nation's wealth continued to increase. The greatest generation paid down debt and their children cranked it up again. After the mid-1970s, governments almost always seem to be running a deficit, as shown in Figure 21.

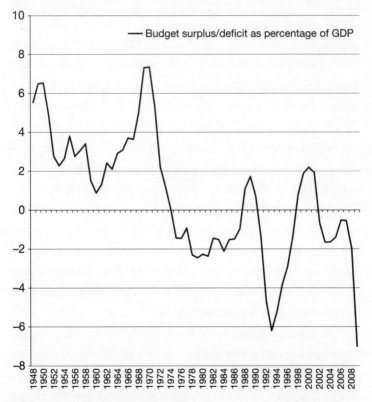

Figure 21. Budget surplus/deficit as a percentage of GDP, 1948–2009 (Office for National Statistics).

But not only did Britain grow the debts it owed; at the same time it received some never-to-be-repeated dividends. As we know, the previous generation sold off, with massive discounts, the very housing that their own parents had struggled to build, but there's more. The discovery and bringing to profit of North Sea oil added an average of 1.7 per cent to GDP in the Thatcher years. Even in 1999, Britain was producing more oil than Iraq, Kuwait or Nigeria.

There was also the privatisation of public utilities, from which government made around £58bn; and, since the shares were effectively subsidised at the point of sale, those who purchased them made an instant 20 per cent profit.[31] Both the Thatcher and Major governments held that Britain should become a share-owning society. Throughout the era, TV adverts like the 'Tell Sid' campaign (which attracted 4.5 million purchasers for British Gas shares) successfully promoted the sale of public utilities to the general public but totally failed to turn Britain into a society of stock-watchers. Share ownership rates actually declined over the Thatcher era. In 1964, before government even thought it a priority, the rate of ownership was 54 per cent. Today, just 10 per cent of the value of shares traded on the UK stock market is held by individuals.[32] Instead, nearly half of the shareholdings in UK companies are now held abroad.[33]

So what happened to all the money? Was the money raised from exploiting communal wealth actually spent for the benefit of future generations? Is there another side to our inheritance? One way to find out is to look at the figures for capital investment, which can be undertaken by private business or the state. In the private sector, Gross Fixed Capital Formation (GFCF) is the not-so-catchy term for money spent on permanent items that businesses need to do their work: buildings, tools, cars. In the public sector, it tots up the money spent on improvements like roads and bridges. It's an ideal measure of the kind of things that can be left behind as inheritance.

In times of plenty and in a low-tax environment, you might have expected companies to actually increase their GFCF, inspired by the thought of future profits and huge success, but that's not what has happened. Between 1970, when it was first measured, and 1980, GFCF averaged 20 per cent of GDP. In the last decade it has fallen to 17 per cent in Britain. When 37 of the wealthiest countries in the world were measured for their capital investment record, Britain came 36th.[34] And when the Institute for Fiscal Studies was asked by the Treasury[35] to find out why, they discovered a big problem: because British companies are often owned by numerous shareholders whose shares are regularly traded, managers are under constant pressure to turn out high profits and dividends, rather than investing some of the profit into the future of the business. What's more, in the modern conception of a corporation, nobody is incentivised to take account of the long-term effects of a lack of investment. Instead, by the time the ill effects of that under-investment are felt by the companies, those who made the decisions are long gone and future employees are left to pick up the pieces.

Exactly the same trend seemed to happen in the public sector – the investment rate fell and has never recovered.

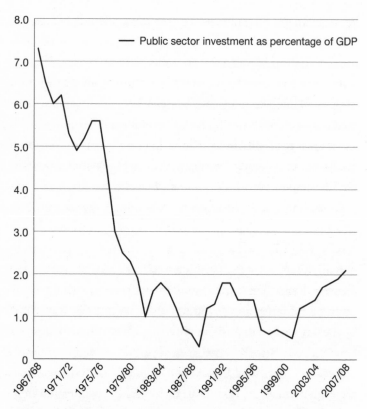

Figure 22. Public-sector investment as a percentage of GDP, 1967–2008 (HM Treasury, 'Public Expenditure Since 1967', in *Public Expenditure Statistical Analyses* (PESA), Chapter 4, 2009).

The reason for the decline is simple: when governments are seeking to reduce their spending, asset investment is always a soft target. Mandarins know it, and we know they know it, because ten years ago the Treasury produced a report into the failure of government to invest in fixed assets since the 1970s. It concluded: 'capital programmes were cut as a way of meeting short-term current pressures, with long-term detrimental effects.'[36]

So can all that money we might have inherited be hidden anywhere else; in secret bank accounts, or under some collective national mattress? Well, there's a single measure that could identify that: net national savings.[37] Unfortunately these have remained at an average of 3 per cent of GDP over the last twenty years,[38] some of the lowest savings figures in the developed world. As Martin Weale says: 'High national debt is a burden on future generations but it would not be if the country had a strong history of past saving. The UK has a very poor history.'

So the wealth hasn't been invested. Nor has it been saved. Perhaps it will come to us in the form of the personal inheritance that so much of the population hates being taxed for. But even when all that's accounted for and folded into the total picture of national inheritance, generational economists believe that our parents' generation – the baby boomers – will leave an average debt for future generations equal to £33,000 each,[39] and this total was calculated in 2005 – two years before the crash. As Weale concludes: 'It is as if the previous generation went on a twenty-year binge.'[40]

Right at the start of this chapter we quoted the chancellor bravely stating that he would stand up for those with that 'most basic human instinct of all', the people who 'aspire to a better life for their children and their grandchildren', and that sounded just grand. But what exactly is the point of an inheritance tax break when the very fundamental costs that any worker joining the economy of Britain deals with – taxation, pensions and investment – are hitting the roof? What use is a tax break when Britain has already been on a 'twenty-year binge' and we're left to deal with the 'long-term detrimental effects'? What use is a personal inheritance if, on average, the jilted generation will each be £33,000 worse off even after it has paid out, and many will receive none in any case? The answer, of course, is that this tax break isn't nearly as meaningful as people think, and certainly not as useful as fixing the underlying problems. The reality of the situation is ignored. But we're not finished here yet.

The members of the jilted generation who *will* inherit, together with their parents who are planning to leave behind an inheritance, might be expecting these resources to counter some of the effects of instability in the housing and jobs markets, as well as the high tax burdens identified in this chapter. They're horribly mistaken. Personal inheritance will offer no quick fix for these problems – because we will inherit too late. On the basis that the baby boomers will live until they are aged between 79 and 84, their children will not receive any inheritance from them for another 20 to 40 years. By that time, many in our generation will simply be too old to reap the benefit: too old to bear children, too old to raise them in a stable environment, too old to enjoy any of those benefits we might assume would be coming our way. An inheritance tax break will offer no security because inheritance itself, for those lucky enough to get it, will come too late.

Meanwhile, in a quest to accrue wealth by keeping taxes low and so build this personal inheritance, long-term investment by businesses and the state seems to have been horrifically neglected. The one-time windfalls of privatisation, North Sea oil, and council house sales have been squandered so fast that we now live in a world that can't even imagine them being there in the first place. Of all these, North Sea oil is particularly striking. Though Britain treated the oil revenues as nothing exceptional – just another income, like taxes, to be squandered accordingly – the Norwegians placed their oil revenues into a sovereign wealth fund that has now grown to £300 billion and will generate wealth and improve the lives of its citizens for years to come. That's an inheritance worth waiting for. Britain's young people, meanwhile, should be hoping their inheritance never happens.

And all this is quite a transformation. Just consider for a second the outlook of our two generations: the baby boomers – richer and better-educated than any before them, with good jobs within reach and family homes waiting around the corner; and the jilted – unstable in work, unstable at home, highly educated but unable to make that education pay, stifled by debt, a generation shackled at birth, in which only those born to parents wealthy enough are likely to prosper.

The purpose of this book has never been to lay the blame for specific and sometimes catastrophic errors at the feet of an entire generation. The need for a banking bail-out can't be blamed on a generation, but is the fault of the stupid and greedy men who believed they could model the repayment of home loans to the poor of North America so accurately that they could insure them, package them and sell them on again at a profit. That no serious provision for state pensions was made by the British government – even when they discovered that the system was unsustainable – is the fault of civil servants and ministers, but not directly of those who are about to claim their pension. Our point is much more straightforward: we will be required to clean up the mess by paying extremely high taxes or receiving fewer of the services on which two previous generations have come to depend. And what will harm us personally will also affect the type of country we pass on to our own children. And the longer we duck the problem, the worse it will get, so we need fixes. We need a different way of doing business, and housing, and debt, and most importantly of all, of doing politics.

But, if we're really going to think seriously about how to do things differently, we must understand how all these bad decisions came about. How is it, for example, that politicians and civil servants forgot about the future? Why, when they did so, was more pressure not brought to bear on them by the rest of society, by the captains of industry, the solemn investors and concerned voters? After all, almost all of them have children themselves. And parents are supposed to be responsible. They aren't supposed to go on 'twenty-year binges'. So what has really been going on?

4

POLITICS

'What we say is save £6 billion in the coming current year in order to stop the jobs tax
which we think will derail the recovery ... I
think we've got to remove this dark cloud of a
deficit over our economy and it makes sense
to make a start on that now. Make a start this
year, to avoid the tax next year, and then we
can go forward with further plans to remove
our deficit and our debt that will hold our
country back if we're not careful.'

David Cameron, first prime ministerial
debate, 15 April 2010

'What David is saying even when it is fragile,
he wants, for ideological reasons I think, to
take £6 billion out of the economy. That puts
thousands of jobs, teachers, it puts policemen,
it puts thousands of jobs at risk immediately,

and that's why they're talking about an emergency budget in June. David, you're a risk to the economy.'

Gordon Brown, second prime ministerial debate, 22 April 2010

'He's supposed to lead this country and he's calling an ordinary woman who's just come up and asked questions what most people would ask him – he's not doing anything about the national debt and it's going to be tax, tax, tax for another twenty years to get out of this national debt – and he's calling me a bigot ...'

Gillian Duffy, Sky News, 28 April 2010

How will history record the 2010 general election? That it produced Britain's first coalition government for 70 years, was the first in which the online media played a pivotal role,[1] and was the first to feature live televised debates between the party leaders are all reasons why it 'changed British politics for good'.[2] Historians might also note that there were some very old-fashioned aspects to the campaign: an almost total lack of high-profile female and minority candidates put forward to represent the parties in print and on television; and problems that continued to dog the polling booths, with at least one constituency running out of ballot papers[3] and dozens more turning away last-minute voters. And the stand-out moment of the campaign occurred in a very traditional setting – far from the burning lights and make-up rooms in the TV debate studios – on the campaign trail in suburban Lancashire on Wednesday 28 April, when someone forgot to turn the prime minister's microphone off.

Gordon Brown's visit to Rochdale was chaotic long before Gillian Duffy arrived. Labour's national campaign managers had arranged the tour at the last minute. The area, a suburb of the town called Healy, was chosen because it had successfully adopted Labour's 'Community Payback Scheme' in which locals decide the punishment for low-level offenders. It was a nice idea, but campaign strategists had failed to notice that the area is also a Liberal Democrat stronghold. Worse, when desperate regional party workers pointed out the error and were advised to go door-to-door to drum up support for Brown on the evening before his visit, they found not a single person keen to meet the prime minister. So, when the sun rose on 28 April, the scene was set for high farce.[4] Brown had already offered a few well-chosen words of encouragement to the criminally-minded of Rochdale serving community sentences on the Payback Scheme when he was introduced to a purposeful lady called Gillian Duffy. Mrs Duffy had lots of questions: how could the prime minister limit immigration, and how was he going to tackle the debt? Brown's answers were flaccid and apologetic; he brought the exchange to an end quickly and dived into his limo. What happened next led the news for the rest of the week.

With a live mic still attached to his jacket, Brown described the visit as 'a disaster' and Mrs Duffy, whose question on immigration he ducked, as a 'bigoted woman'. The recording was played, almost on a loop, across all news channels for days afterwards. It was further evidence, said Britain's commentators, of the prime minister's personal weakness and ill temper, perhaps even of the contempt Britain's politicians hold for the general public.

The exchange was important for another reason. Moments after Mrs Duffy heard the insulting recording, she explained why she had approached the prime minister in the first place: 'I thought, well I'll ask him, "What is he going to do about the national debt?" ... When he was chancellor he did very good things for this country, but now it's all gone to pot, everything. And you've got to sort it out, else your grandchildren, your children will be paying for all this debt.'

Mrs Duffy had chosen to raise the most pressing issue facing Britain – the debt that the jilted generation will spend our lives repaying. And she wasn't the only one to realise it. One day earlier, the director of the Institute for Fiscal Studies, Robert Chote, had made the same point: 'Given that a fiscal repair job is likely to be the major domestic policy challenge for the next government,' he said, 'it is striking how reticent all three main UK parties have been in explaining how they would confront the task.'

As the campaign progressed, things got no clearer. Instead, the Tories talked about cutting £6bn from public spending to tackle the debt and cancel out a small rise in National Insurance proposed by Brown, Labour claimed that this would endanger the nation's economic recovery, and the Liberal Democrats proposed £15bn of public-sector cuts, but mostly to pay for lower tax rates. Not one of them stated the plain facts.

The Tories wanted to cut deeper to cut the debt quickly, but this could endanger recovery by placing thousands of public servants on the dole – with obvious implications for Treasury receipts and consumer spending. Meanwhile, Labour's plan, to keep spending levels high, would probably mean raising taxes more aggressively than they claimed – with obvious implications for the struggling businesses that would be forced to pay them. And, since the debt is so vast, whoever won the election would probably be required to both raise taxes and cut spending in any event. Both sides knew the score, not only because they are economically literate but because the governor of the Bank of England said so: 'Whoever wins this election will be out of power for a whole generation because of how tough the fiscal austerity will have to be.'[5] But both Brown and Cameron refused to admit reality.

Instead they began a kind of weird dance in which both sides refused to reveal the hard details of what would need to be done to rescue the economy. This is how it worked: the Conservative party claimed to want to cut just £6bn, which they considered to be such a small sum that it could not reasonably be said to endanger the economy (nor, though, could it meaningfully cut the deficit), but they refused to release much more detailed information about other cuts, fearful that Labour would use this as a stick to beat them. The Labour party, meanwhile, refused to talk about tax rises so the Tories couldn't pin them down either. Both sides refused to state what tax rises or spending cuts they really wanted to make, and neither plan really worked – Labour still said the Tories were 'a risk to the recovery', the Tories still said that Labour tax plans would stop growth.

To Gillian Duffy this seemed confusing, to Robert Chote it looked ridiculous; in truth it was a conspiracy of the cowardly: Britain's politicians refused to honestly tell voters how they would tackle the debt in case their true position was unpopular. And so no voter could make an objective decision based on the facts. And, deep down, we all knew it – not just those in the know, eminent economists like Chote, but the rest of us, including Mrs Duffy. What's more, once the formality of a democratic election was completed, the Tory-led coalition got down to business and pressed for the very cuts the party refused to discuss in the campaign. If anything, their justifications for this were even more ridiculous. On 7 June 2010, David Cameron wrote a bouncy email to Tory activists with his bizarre justification for the action he wanted to take but dared not admit to the electorate:

> I've been spending a lot of time with Ministers and officials, discussing the big challenges facing Britain and what we've got to do to sort them out. What we didn't know for sure before is how much the interest on our debt is likely to rise in the years to come. We didn't know this because the last government refused to publish the information. Now we've got the figure, I can see why they tried to keep it secret. So what's the figure? Well, if we carry on as we

are, in five years time the interest we will pay
on our debt could be around £70 billion.[6]

This justification for making spending cuts and tax rises that
were never put to the electorate is pure fiction – a determined
misrepresentation of what we knew. This £70bn was known.
It had already been calculated from the figures released in
Labour chancellor Alistair Darling's budget in March 2010.
For the current prime minister to use this 'secret' as the excuse
to cut government spending looks pretty thin.

In an era of expenses scandals and dodgy dossiers, the
news that politicians play fast and loose with the truth isn't
exactly unexpected. But in some ways the fake debate on debt
is even more scandalous than these, since it wasn't buried in
parliamentary accounts ready for a crack team of journalists
to uncover, nor in reports released half-way through a parliament, but was faked at the very moment when voters get a say
about the shape of their country.

During times of recession, choices get harder and the
cost of brutal honesty with the electorate gets higher. Some
might say that no sensible politician would broach the subject
of the debt with cold rationality and expect to win. But the
really curious thing about British politics in the last decade
is that even in the good times politicians have failed to own
up to what they really think, and why, on all sorts of subjects
– drugs, immigration, terrorism. But among the unmentiona-
bles of British politics one issue stands out: the future.

Whether it's the housing problems or the job shortages
that now plague Britain's young people, or the nation's debts

– both implicit and explicit – the same observation can be made: these problems have been created by politicians failing to act in Britain's long-term interests. In some cases the future consequences of decisions are difficult to predict; that globalisation would depress wages and create job insecurity was perhaps not immediately obvious to those who championed it. But of all our problems, right now, national debt is the most palpable; its cost hits Britain every year with dramatic and obvious consequences for taxpayers and the public sector, yet even this wasn't seriously addressed. So why were all the issues that will shape the lives of members of the jilted generation seemingly pushed aside at the election?

Some people might say that young people have only themselves to blame, that if they were more politically active they would be able to re-tilt the scales; but this, of course, isn't how it works. When, before the 2005 general election, the Electoral Commission launched a campaign to persuade young people to vote with the shout-line: 'If you don't do politics … there's not much you do do', they missed the point entirely. It's not that young people don't do politics, it's that modern politics doesn't do young people.

Old people power

While our interests tend to be ignored, our parents, and those older than them, received a whole tranche of specific pledges from the three main parties. They include: free TV licences for those over 75; protected winter fuel payments – these are given irrespective of need, by the way, so even millionaires get the perks; no changes to the default retirement age for anyone over 60; restoring the earnings link for the state pension from 2011; and increases in NHS spending. We're just not part of the political calculation while our parents are, so what's going on?

As the myriad of policies targeted at our parents' generation but not at us suggest, politicians are more interested in their vote than ours. Just take a look at two speeches made by David Cameron soon after he was made leader of the Tory party. Both were given in October 2006, the first in front of an audience drawn from the charity Age Concern, now Age UK, the second to the Young Adult Trust.

In the first speech, Cameron chose to dismiss Blair's 'Cool Britannia' era: 'Only the new, the young and the modern could be part of the picture of Britain he wanted to paint. It was absurd. He even said "This is a young country" – it isn't. The fact is we are an old country – with our best years ahead of us.' And the Tory leader went on to explain that the baby boomers had a vital role to play in society and could count on his help; that his objection to modern development was that it provided 'less room for elderly parents' – though, as we know, the real problem is that there's less room for young couples who want to start families; that he favoured lower taxes for pensioners; that 'older people are active and forward-looking participants in society'.[7]

In the room full of young people who watched the second speech, Cameron, perhaps scarred by his 'hug a hoodie' talk earlier in the year, was careful to emphasise 'responsibilities' and talk rather less about equivalent 'rights' for our age group: no TV licence giveaways here: 'Of course there are some things – like the right to vote, or the age of criminal responsibility – which have to be fixed by age', he explained. 'But in most things, it's not about age. It's about responsibility. And that's the real reason we need to change the way we hand out rights and duties. Because we need to do far more to promote responsibility.'[8]

Of course, the message was correct – it is important for young people to take responsibility for their actions – but the difference in the speeches was one of emphasis: young people must shape up, old people should be valued more highly.

Nor has this kind of pro-elderly approach been confined to Tory politics. In the same week as Cameron made those speeches, Labour work and pensions secretary John Hutton wrote a memo to the Labour party chair, Hazel Blears, calling for a new campaign to appeal specifically to our parents' generation: 'In many of our marginal seats, the baby boomers could make a decisive difference at the next election', he pronounced, before adding, crawlingly, 'the baby boomers are actually the altruistic generation.'[9]

For David Willetts, the Tory minister for science and higher education who worked hard in opposition to highlight the generational divide, this kind of posturing is, perhaps, evidence of politicians being 'susceptible to political pressure'[10] from the baby boomers. But if there is 'political pressure', it tends not to be overt. There's no baby boomer political party or pressure group that pushes their agenda. You won't find anyone in Westminster calling themselves the 'minister for baby boomers'. Indeed, Britain is no longer led by a baby boomer prime minister. But you don't need a government led by one particular age group to appeal to that group – it will happen quite naturally when politicians are attempting to take their votes, and that's precisely what they're doing. They've looked at the numbers and what they've discovered is that baby boomers are much more likely to vote than young people.

In the 2010 general election, 50 per cent of young people aged between 18 and 34 turned out to vote, while 75 per cent of those aged 55 and over entered the polling booth.[11] And not only are baby boomers much more likely to vote, but, as we know, there are also many more of them than us. In the run-up to the 2005 election, MORI calculated that the over-55s had 4.2 times the voting power of 18- to 34-year-olds.[12]

Of course, not all of these people vote the same way, but politicians from all parties, eager to get baby boomer votes, have become prone to paying them special attention, giving them special favours. And, of course, these favours might not merely include the odd free TV licence, but also the decision to encourage housing speculation of the kind that has locked young people out of the housing market as we described in Chapter 1, or the championing of post-retirement working while millions of young people are unemployed as we described in Chapter 2. Suddenly, it's possible to perceive a skewing of policy away from the interests of the jilted generation and towards those of their parents – not by any conscious effort by voters, but simply because of the numbers. No wonder, therefore, that when David Willetts first spoke about the role of demographics in British society he concluded: 'A young person could be forgiven for seeing Britain's economic and political structure as nothing less than a conspiracy by the baby boomers in our own interests.'[13]

Do the baby boomers secretly control British politics?

If this is true in the last few years of British politics, is it possible that there have been similar effects in earlier years? It is, for example, notable that the pattern of inflation – dramatically influenced by government decisions – seemed to work in cycle with baby boomer preferences. When the baby boomers purchased houses in the 1970s and 1980s, they enjoyed very high inflation, which cut the cost of their mortgages. They have enjoyed very low inflation in the last decade as they have grown old and sought to build up their savings. But could it also be the case that the effect of this huge generation is even deeper and broader than this? Might the high level of government debt that Britain now wrestles, might the instability that young people now face, might even that fake debate at the 2010 general election actually all have come about because of the baby boomers?

At first sight those questions seem outlandish, and certainly different from the narrative that we have been told about the baby boomers who were all hippies building a glorious new utopia. When you think about when they were young, you immediately think of 'the swinging sixties', spliffs, sex and subversion. And, if you look at it more closely, didn't that sixties and seventies generation achieve massive social change for which we can all be grateful? Certainly the legislation passed in those decades would suggest so. In 1967 homosexuality was decriminalised, a year later the rules on censorship in the theatre were relaxed. In 1970 the Equal Pay Act gave women legal protection from discrimination at work and the voting age was lowered to eighteen. How could these people have damaged the prospects of young people?

Many would argue they have not; that their legacy has been nothing short of splendid. The boomers have concocted a near-mythological narrative of their youth, of rallies and riots, ideology and idolatry, which many of them claim changed the face of British society. They claim responsibility for establishing female equality, fighting discrimination and, in general, making Britain a more green, fair and free nation. Aspects of this mythology can be found everywhere – from the cottage industry of self-help books and memoirs pushed out by boomers like Rosie Boycott (*A Nice Girl Like Me: A Story of the Seventies*) and Esther Rantzen (*If Not Now, When? Living the Baby Boomer Adventure*), to the almost perpetual re-issuing of baby boomer cultural emblems, be they Che Guevara T-shirts or Warhol retrospectives or Stones albums. For many, the era of the mid-1960s represented a break from the past. The core theme of the age was to break down the stuffy 'Edwardian establishment' against which Harold Wilson would later rage. It was a theme that seeped into every aspect of the era, from Kenneth Tynan's review of *Look Back In Anger*, which revealed 'post war youth as it really is, the instinctive leftishness, the sense of humour, the classlessness',[14] to descriptions of Lord Snowdon in *Newsweek*: 'Tony is impatient with pomp.'[15] The restricting walls of Britain's gloomy post-war society were to be scaled and smashed by a new generation. As Christopher Booker records in his biography of the decade:

> The word classless could be guaranteed to appear in any article about the New Aristocrats [the most fashionable young people in the mid-1960s] ... The collective image was one of revolt against 'old-fashioned', 'bourgeois convention'. The press was delighted, for instance, with David Bailey's wedding to French actress Catherine Deneuve, when, as the *Evening Standard* put it, 'The bridegroom wore a light-blue sweater ... and light green corduroy trousers, the bride arrived smoking'.[16]

And if this youth movement was essentially 'classless', elements of it would soon develop more overtly political characteristics to challenge class. Marxism was the vogue, as the former student radical and political polemicist Tariq Ali explained in a 2008 article on the 1968 protests against the Vietnam War: 'We believed – and still do – that people should not be measured by material possessions but by their ability to transform the lives of others – the poor and underprivileged; that the economy needed to be reorganised in the interests of the many, not the few; and that socialism without democracy could never work. Above all, we believed in freedom of speech.'[17]

The movement was variously called a 'counter-culture' and a 'rock revolution' with mood music penned by the biggest bands in the world. It produced a profusion of pamphleteering, magazines, demonstrations and festivals, all of which were the mechanisms by which these young radicals would 'stick it to the man'. And there was strong evidence that they would succeed.

Even before the Grosvenor Square riots against US involvement in Vietnam, Paul Johnson, while deputy editor of the *New Statesman* magazine, wrote an article in 1964 about the growing power of the boomers, entitled 'The Menace of Beatlism': 'Bewildered by a rapidly changing society, excessively fearful of becoming out of date, our leaders are increasingly turning to young people as guides and mentors – or, to vary the metaphor, as Geiger counters to guide them against the perils of mental obsolescence.'[18]

It was certainly true that our parents' generation were treated differently by their political leaders than we are. In that same year, 1964, Harold Wilson had been making opportunistic speeches about 'change' (sound familiar?): 'Change for resurgence,' he said, 'and to refit Britain with a new image … we are living in the jet-age but we are governed by an Edwardian establishment mentality.' Wilson wanted 'the youth of Britain' with their 'thrusting ability' and 'iconoclasm' to 'storm the frontiers of knowledge'.[19] There was no mention of David Cameron's 'responsibilities' in these speeches.

Instead, Wilson had recognised that to win elections, he would be wise to harness the voting power of young people too. But even if there's some evidence to suggest that baby

boomers have been playing a dominant role in British politics for decades, it doesn't explain why the jilted generation is
afflicted by poor housing and job prospects and high debts,
let alone why the 2010 election played host to that cowardly
and dishonest debate about debt – not least because, as Tariq
Ali says, the mores of that generation were so righteous.

In fact, Ali's narrative of the role of his generation of political activists is slightly different to this. What he says is that
the 'rock revolutionaries' lost; that things began to fall apart
and the political movements of the late 1960s and 1970s were
ultimately undermined and destroyed: 'During the last two
decades of the 20th century the world was turned upside
down again', he has written. 'As each alternative to its rule
crumbled into dust, Capital and its worshippers celebrated a
victory that seemed definitive. For the left it was a defeat of
historic proportions. Utopia was erased from the map of the
world.'[20]

This view is common. Even in 1969, leading baby-boomer
commentators like Germaine Greer saw the writing on the
wall: 'The rock revolution failed because it was corrupted. It
was incorporated in the capitalist system which has power to
absorb and exploit all tendencies, including the tendencies
towards its own overthrow.'[21]

The 'man', an inchoate enemy – embodied for many in
the disgraced US president Richard Nixon – had won. The
revolution was over and the great social changes that one
unique generation had wrought on Britain began to slow
down. Except, of course, they hadn't and they didn't. The
truth is that Ali and Greer's notion of the 'swinging sixties'

youth of the baby boomers and their political and social revolution is mythology. It's a bedtime story they tell themselves about their heady, radical, world-changing youth.

The idea that a generation could all come together as 'agents of change' doesn't hold up to scrutiny. Self-evidently not all the baby boomers were Marxist, not all were members of the New Aristocracy, and very few participated in the 'rock revolution'. Political radicalism didn't emerge as a kind of logical conclusion of rock and roll as Greer implies. The assumption made by mythologists of the 1960s was that a single generation came together to reshape Britain, but that didn't happen. A population spike isn't to blame for the fake debate on debt in the 2010 election, any more than it's responsible for job instability. And nor, for that matter, is the failure of Ali's political movement. No, to really understand why Britain's politicians forgot about the long term and became almost pathologically unable to hold serious opinions about the future, we're going to have to turn elsewhere, to the values that have shaped the modern world. To understand these values we need to look again at the post-war period and the baby boomers who were brought up in it. What we argue is that the boomer mythology has obscured the really big change: the dawning of a new age of self-expression and the spread of a philosophy of individualism that completely reshaped Britain's politics. It's these trends that explain many of our generation's problems; that explain our housing crisis and our low wages and unemployment; that even explain why we got that fake debate on debt. And our story doesn't begin in Grosvenor Square or at Glastonbury, but before the baby boomers were born.[22]

How individualism reshaped Britain

In the late 1940s, two groups of people who seemed new and very strange appeared for the first time in Britain. The first, united by their music, were a tiny cult of young men determined to revive the jazz styles that began in Chicago in the 1920s. Led by artists like George Melly and Humphrey Lyttelton, they were unconventional public school boys with a very distinct take on what music was 'cool'. The second group, united by their clothing, were teenagers raised in the poorest areas of south London who, seemingly for no good reason, began to dress in long Edwardian coats and drainpipe trousers. They were collectively known as Teddy Boys. Both groups were young; both saw themselves as distinct from conventional society and all the more romantic for that. And they were the first manifestations of a 'youth culture' that would later be gripped by the satire boom of the late 1950s, fall in love with The Beatles in the early 1960s, protest with Tariq Ali at the end of that decade, and lead a 'counter-culture' in the years that followed. All of these different age groups would have something in common, but it wasn't 'the music', nor 'the politics', nor even 'the culture'. Instead, they were the first generation in our society who were free, educated,[23] and, in the booming post-war economy, relatively rich. And in a constrained and class-ridden society, they desperately wanted to express themselves.[24] How this educated, mobile and creative generation and those that followed them would realise this ambition is vital to understanding why we are where we are today.

Back in the 1950s, academics and commentators were quick enough to note that Britain now had a 'youth culture', but it wasn't until the end of that decade that the behaviour of these youths would be systematically examined. In 1959 Mark Abrams published a book based on his analysis of consumption trends and polling information. He called it *The Teenage Consumer* and argued in it that young people were intensely preoccupied with discovering their identities and consuming products that were 'emotionally-charged'.[25] He said that teenagers were not rational but had unique 'teenage' patterns of consumption,[26] and he saw this consumption intrinsically linked to 'working-class consumerism' which had begun much earlier but which found meaningful expression in the post-war environment through the growth of hire-purchase schemes of ownership. His observations had dramatic implications. For, if the young 'working classes' were now major consumers, they would inevitably – and for the first time – begin to shape Britain's culture through their buying habits.

At that time the discussion of the 'classless society' was, as previously noted, becoming a fixation of commentators and young radicals, and Abrams's book only added fuel to the discussion. Serious new works of analysis were undertaken, exploring how power was exercised in Britain, and by whom. The *Spectator* magazine attempted to define young people's 'radicalism' against the old elites, while the historian Hugh Thomas edited a book exploring 'the establishment' – that shadowy network of great institutions really running British society and which, some argued, was holding back the creativity of its people. The writings of the Italian Marxist Antonio Gramsci, which set out to describe a 'hegemony' in which one ruling class runs a society for its own benefit, became hugely popular. But contrary to what Ali and others might suggest, Gramsci wasn't the only show in town.

In 1957 an academic called Richard Hoggart wrote *The Uses of Literacy*, in which he suggested that the forces of political radicalism and baby-boomer insurgency were a red herring. Instead, the rise of consumerism itself would change Britain's communities – particularly for the working class. 'The great majority of us are being merged into one class',[27] he wrote, before explaining that British culture was undergoing a process of what he called 'massification'. This was the mechanism by which metropolitan advertisers and the national media were robbing localities of their individuality and people within them of inherited values. As a result, Hoggart argued, the individuals of the future would become: 'Riddled with a fuzzy form of egalitarianism, ridden with doubt and self-doubt, believing nothing and able to honour almost no one; in such circumstances we stand on nothing and so can stand for nothing.'[28]

What Hoggart predicted was how the new 'emotional' products and the mindset that flowed from interaction with them would reshape our society. There was, of course, a political movement in the decade that followed the publication of his book. But this 'counter-cultural' movement, led by the young vanguard intent on breaking down class barriers in society, was not what it seemed. What was important was the self-expression, not necessarily what was said. And that meant the movement could be commodified. As a result, big business quickly learned that the 'Summer of Love', 'flower power' and the anti-capitalist rage of the baby boomers would present a marvellous business opportunity.

The process by which counter-culture would become over-the-counter-culture was almost too slow to notice. Though some companies – notably Dagenham-based Ford Motors – worked hard throughout the 1960s to market their products towards young people, it wasn't until the end of the decade that large corporations attempted to scientifically understand what motivated them. The process began in the United States. There, life-insurance companies had become panicked by the fact that US baby boomers had stopped buying their services – they simply couldn't understand it. So the US Institute of Life Insurance asked Daniel Yankelovich to find the answer and, in 1970, he produced *Finance-Related Attitudes of Youth*,[29] the first really serious attempt to understand what motivated the baby boom generation.

In an interview completed decades later, Yankelovich explained what he found: 'The life insurance business was built on the Protestant ethic. You only bought life insurance if you were a person who sacrificed for the future. They had some sense that the values of the Protestant ethic were being challenged by the new values that were starting to appear and I was really astonished by what I found. The conventional, dominant interpretation was that it had to do with political radicalism. It was clear to us that that was a mask, a cover; the core of it had to do with self-expressiveness. This preoccupation with the inner self – that was what was so important to people.'[30]

Four years later, in 1974, Yankelovich asked young people to define their 'primary aims'. Given a list of four choices – a happy family, a fulfilling career, making a lot of money, or the opportunity to develop as an individual – 45 per cent chose the final category. Perhaps that doesn't seem so remarkable now, but wait. Yankelovich asked the same question of Americans drawn from all age groups. The result speaks for itself: just 12 per cent picked the opportunity to develop as an individual. Eighty per cent said a happy family life was most important.[31]

In both 1970 and 1974, the survey asked the extent of agreement with this statement: 'People sacrifice too much for their children; they should put more emphasis on themselves.' The 1974 report concluded: 'Young people's overall agreement has remained at the same level over the four years, but intensity of feeling on the subject, particularly disagreement, has diminished.'[32]

What Yankelovich had discovered is that these new citizens were consumers but they wanted products that would express their individuality. 'A particular music system, your clothing, these become ways in which people can spend their money in order to say who they are', explained Yankelovich. 'In 1970, [the prime desire to be individual] was just a small percentage of the population, maybe three to five per cent. By 1980, it had spread to up to eighty per cent.'

These new desires were going to require very new ways of marketing products. Traditionally, advertising was designed to offer products that would 'solve a problem' – buy a chair if you need to sit down, buy a coat if you're cold – and advertising focused on how individual products could offer a solution. However, if people weren't interested in merely 'solving problems' but expressing themselves, this made advertising much more difficult because corporations had no way of knowing how people wanted to express themselves.

A solution to this problem was finally devised by Stanford Research Institute (SRI), where a technique for accurately targeting the self-expressive new individuals was developed, called 'VALs' – 'Values And Lifestyles'. VALs was really the first major shift towards the modern multi-billion-dollar consumer research industry.[33] And the object of a VALs survey was not to discover what a consumer needed so much as who they wanted to be, by examining their social values. VALs researchers drew a distinction between traditional consumers and the new baby boomer expressive consumers whom they called the 'inner-directed'. What VALs could do was understand very specifically who they were and what their values stood for, and that allowed companies to market their products to them, not on the basis of what those products could do but on the basis of how they would make them feel.

By the late 1970s SRI had taken their techniques over to the UK, where falling consumer demand and industrial action were crippling the domestic economy. Soon British as well as American companies began to sell all kinds of products that were 'emotionally-charged', as Abrams put it, that didn't just satisfy a function but expressed the purchaser's feelings and lifestyle. And this trend remains with us today. Indeed, almost all of the most successful new products that have been marketed to people in the last 30 years have attempted to do just that. The marketing of these brands often has little to do with the core product they make or sell but is specifically designed to create emotional expressive attachment.[34] As Naomi Klein says in her book *No Logo*, brands have become the single most valuable part of any company because they summon the emotional attachment that consumers have with a particular product – be it Apple, Coca-Cola or Mars.

Back in the late 1970s, the market researchers realised that VALs might have applications far beyond the selling of products. They noticed that the language used by Margaret Thatcher, and in the US by Ronald Reagan, about the freedom of individuals was exactly what their 'inner-directed' new consumers wanted to hear.

In 1975, Thatcher told the Conservative party conference: 'Some Socialists seem to believe that people should be numbers in a State computer. We believe they should be individuals. We are all unequal. No one, thank heavens, is like anyone else, however much the Socialists may pretend otherwise. We believe that everyone has the right to be unequal but to us every human being is equally important.'

The inner-directed generation, obsessed with expressing themselves, were certainly seduced. As Christine MacNulty, the UK VALs programme manager, stated in an interview years later: 'It was the inner-directeds who said that they would vote for Thatcher and for Reagan and they made the difference in those elections.'[35]

And not only did VALs research show that, but so do the actual voting statistics: in 1979 Margaret Thatcher received a 16 per cent swing in support from young people aged 18–35 – the baby boomers – significantly more than any other group,[36] and they made up more than one third of the electorate. Without their support she wouldn't have gained power. This story is very different from the one put across by the baby boomer revolutionaries in Britain. Far from being defeated by some kind of conspiracy of global capitalism, the baby boomers themselves voted in Thatcher – the apotheosis of a capitalist prime minister.

However, VALs research also gives far more information about what happened to those 'inner-directed' boomers after 1979. In an interview with the authors, Pat Breman, a member of the modern VALs Strategic Insight Team in the US, explained: 'We noticed that the primary motivation for self-expression identified in the baby boomers began to morph in the early 1980s over a period of ten to fifteen years. They had started off as quite values-driven people but they became really interested in the achievement of success and status.'[37]

And this makes perfect sense. If individuals are able to use brands and lifestyle products to express themselves, then you might expect them to treat with increasing importance those brands and their involvement with them. What's more, since Thatcher's economic policies were designed to keep taxes low and give people more money to spend on these products, you might expect them to be popular too – since if a person had more money they could express themselves even more effectively.

How individualism remade politics

As we described in Chapter 2, the Thatcher years created a kind of paradigm shift in economic terms, not least because they created a consumer boom that has never really slowed down. However, Thatcher's motivation for using the language of freedom and self-expression wasn't some cynical calculation to win votes. She wasn't a baby boomer, but a hardworking, self-reliant and independent woman, a grocer's daughter who rose to the top of politics. And at the heart of her policies was a fundamental assumption about the nature of society drawn from her own experience: individuals know what they want better than anyone else, and it's foolish to attempt to command Britain's resources on their behalf when they can tell much better what's good for them. Further, individual freedom is best enabled by free-market capitalism. This particular view of the world had further significance during the long-running Cold War stand-off with Russia, where individual freedom had been almost completely supplanted by state control. In 1988 Thatcher gave an interview to *Woman's Own* magazine in which she laid out exactly what she believed: 'I think we have gone through a period when too many children and people have been given to understand "I have a problem, it is the Government's job to cope with it!" or "I have a problem, I will go and get a grant to cope with it!" "I am homeless, the Government must house me!" and so they are casting their problems on society, and who is society?

There is no such thing! There are individual men and women and there are families, and no government can do anything except through people and people look to themselves first.'[38]

Thatcher's rationale wasn't merely based on gut feeling, though. By the time she came to office she could rely on theories developed over decades by an array of international thinkers and activists. They included Karl Popper, James M. Buchanan and Milton Friedman, but chief among them was the Austrian philosopher Friedrich von Hayek, who formed the Mont Pelerin Society of which they were all members. The Society, named after the Swiss spa at which they met, released a founding statement in 1947 lamenting the 'decline of belief in private property and the competitive free market' and warning that 'the individual and the voluntary group are progressively undermined by extensions of arbitrary power'.[39]

Each member of the group violently disagreed with the idea that the state should pull the levers of the economy, as happened during the post-war period in Britain. But this notion garnered little support among politicians and economists busy building a comprehensive system of welfare and expanding the remit of government to make society 'fairer'. However, the levers of centralised economic control began to stop working when both unemployment and inflation rose rapidly and at the same time in the 1970s. This wasn't supposed to happen, and it couldn't be explained by the economic theories followed by those politicians. The 'neo-liberals' were waiting in the wings with answers to the problem. They believed that government must curtail its activities. Their conceptions – monetarism, public choice theory, the small state – sought to rebuild the economy around the 'individual' who knew their own mind and, in a free market, could make better decisions for themselves than government could make on their behalf. It followed that to be free and to be successful, government must get out of the way. This wasn't just about efficiency, it was about justice. As Milton Friedman, the architect of monetarism, wrote in 1980:

> A society that puts equality – in the sense of equality of outcome – ahead of freedom will end up with neither equality nor freedom. The use of force to achieve equality will destroy freedom, and the force, introduced for good purposes, will end up in the hands of those who use it to promote their own interests.[40]

Many of Thatcher's policies – the deregulation of the City of London, council house sales and privatisation – followed the neo-liberals' credo: it wasn't society's job to stand in the way of individuals, nor was it government's job to maintain infrastructure and businesses that were inefficient. It was certainly not government's job to ensure full employment either, because how many people should be employed, and in what way and for what remuneration, was a question for the individuals running businesses, not for the state. And to a great extent, Thatcher and her Conservative supporters believed that this view of the world was vindicated by its results. Britain's GDP skyrocketed throughout the late 1980s and

1990s and at the same time the dominant alternative system – communism – was collapsing in Russia.

But this conception of society also owed much to those discussions of 'classlessness' that occurred twenty years earlier. Some of those young radicals who had sought to define and expose 'the establishment' now gathered around Thatcher. Hugh Thomas, who had edited the selection of essays on the subject, became chairman of Thatcher's pet think-tank, the Centre for Policy Studies, in the year she came to power. Under him worked a former communist named Sir Alfred Sherman who was described by one colleague as a man who 'doesn't like institutions', and 'institutions don't like him'.[41] Sherman hated the establishment and argued vociferously that establishment civil servants threatened Thatcher's mission. In common with the other radical neo-liberals around Thatcher, both men saw their job as to weaken the establishment; and to do this, they would use exactly the same mechanisms and theories that Thatcher put into practice in the economy, only this time they would be aimed at the heart of government itself.

For example, 'public choice theory' explained that all public servants used their positions to acquire power and resources rather than serve the public good.[42] James M. Buchanan, one of the leading academics associated with the Mont Pelerin Society, posed the following question: 'On what rational grounds can the individual decide that a particular activity belongs to a realm of social as opposed to private choices?'[43] He argued that there's no rational difference between social and private activity when democracies function effectively, and that constitutions should be structured in such a way that the self-interests of all public employees should work in harmony with the efficient use of resources. This thinking stood in firm opposition to the long-held view of public service in Britain, and particularly that of the civil service with its ethos that the people who work for it 'are more concerned with jobs where they can help other people and which are useful to society'.[44] Buchanan labelled this ethos 'romantic and illusory';[45] Sir Alfred Sherman would probably have described it as the self-justification of a self-serving elite. In any case, one of the major reforming actions of the Thatcher government was to attempt to expose this hypocrisy and bring civil servants into line. The number of civil servants was cut by around a third during her time in office, the Civil Service Department was abolished and merged with the Cabinet Office, and reforms led by the former chief executive of Marks and Spencer, Derek Rayner, attempted to ensure that Whitehall 'mandarins' focused more on driving efficiency than deciding policy. Further, in order that public servants' duties to the public and their self-interests could be aligned, the Thatcher government introduced incentives for cost-cutting and rewards for efficient work.[46]

The public-choice theorists had a second and related observation to share with Britain's free-market governments based on their assumptions about self-interested individuals. They argued that democracy itself is not very good at processing information and getting good results, for a whole set of reasons. These include the powerlessness of individual voters and the range of factors they must account for in their single vote (party, leader, MP, manifesto, etc.). Buchanan said that a much better information-processor was the free market. As a result, John Major's government attempted to change how people interacted with the public sector to mimic their experiences as consumers in the private sector – in the free market. By doing so, Major believed he would finally tear down the elites that were holding Britain back. He called this, in an echo of those 1960s debates, his vision for a 'classless society'.

The Major government created the 'Citizens' Charter', a programme designed to take ten years and which, said the former prime minister, would 'find better ways of converting money into better services'.[47] League tables were created for school examination results and council performance, NHS patients were given guaranteed time limits for consultations, and even railway passengers were offered money back when their trains ran late. In this way the performance of public servants could be measured scientifically. There would be no escape for the self-interested bureaucrats.

Under New Labour these ideas were pushed even further. In April 1997 – one month before Labour was elected to power – Tony Blair delivered an angry election broadcast based on the idea that 'Britain can be better'. In it, the future prime minister explicitly conceded that many of the reforms of the Thatcher era had worked, and stated that if things were to improve, bureaucracy needed to be cut further and taxes should not rise. The Thatcherite model of politics had been endorsed by the Labour party:

> Look, the Tories didn't get everything wrong
> in the 1980s. Let's just be honest about that
> and admit it, but Britain can be better … The
> Tories today are no longer the party of low
> taxes. The fact is they broke their word on
> taxes. The fact is they raised taxes 22 times.
> Ordinary families have had 22 tax rises under
> the Conservatives – the most in peacetime
> history. Now, I don't want to add to those
> tax rises … We've got to rebuild the National
> Health Service and as a start we will spend
> £100m by cutting that bureaucracy and
> putting it into cutting waiting lists.[48]

What Blair recognised, just as Major had done, was the power
of individualism. He said later, in yet another echo of that
same sixties language, what motivated him and his party:
'New Labour, confident at having modernised itself, is now
the new progressive force in British politics which can mod-
ernise the nation, sweep away those forces of conservatism to
set the people free.'[49]

And he would follow precisely the same policy that Major
had adopted to build his 'classless society' – targets and
incentives. In 1998 David Blunkett offered head teachers a 10
per cent bonus if they met the condition of what he called 'a
tough new appraisal system'; and in 2003 the NHS adopted a
'payment by results framework' for managers and, later, general practitioners. In 2006 Blair told social workers: 'We will
incentivise good practice.'[50] But the power of incentives could

be extended far beyond the civil service; he even talked of incentivising couples to have children.[51]

The Thatcher, Major and Blair administrations were operating policies of government that, deep down, were based on the idea that all individuals are self-interested and motivated purely by money, and that any claim they have to 'public service' or duty or ethical behaviour is a cover story or, worse, mere emotion that blinds them to their own interests.

There is, of course, another possibility. It might just be that many public servants really do choose their careers because they believe in helping society. It's interesting to note that the politicians who have followed public choice theories tend not to have been able to speak plainly about them in public because their root observations concerning the motives of public servants are hardly likely to win votes. It would have been impossible for Thatcher or even Blair to tell teachers, nurses or doctors that they are motivated only by money, that they do their work for self-interested reasons, that only by aligning their personal aims with the public good will lives be saved or children educated – and yet these were the ideas that informed their policies. So, let's return to the original question right at the start of the chapter: why are Britain's political parties failing to be honest about how they tackle the problems facing our generation? Here we begin to get a shape of an answer – it may be that they are failing because some of the most basic assumptions upon which modern government is founded are unpalatable. And they've grown used to holding back what they really think.

In an era of expenses scandals and public-sector fat-cattery, it's easy to sympathise with those public service-bashing policies, and they were popular in the 1980s. One of the reasons for the success of the BBC's much-loved *Yes Minister* series was that it seemed to accurately portray politicians and civil servants in a constant battle over their own interests while the interests of the public were flatly ignored. This has the ring of truth. Anyone who has been shabbily treated by state employees has felt it – and we've all been treated shabbily at one time or another. But there are several ways in which the problem identified in the *Yes Minister* series can be addressed. One way would be to ensure that fewer decisions are made by Whitehall and far more by local political bodies. Generally speaking, decisions are best made as near as possible to the people they affect. However, in the case of both Major and Blair, their response to the problem posed by public servants was not to decentralise power but to do the exact opposite.

By setting almost limitless targets and incentives, almost all public servants were tied into even more bureaucratic and centralised systems of management. And, crudely administered, the targets had vast and absurd unintended consequences. In the field of healthcare the results were particularly extreme. For example, when NHS managers were set targets to reduce waiting lists, some forced consultants to prioritise easy operations that could be completed quickly while more serious ones – like cancer operations – were pushed into the background. One study even found that two thirds of English hospitals cancelled operations and diverted staff and beds from other departments in those weeks when A&E waiting-time targets were inspected.[52] At the start of 2010, the government report into the Mid Staffordshire NHS Foundation Trust – Britain's worst, where 1,200 more people died of neglect and botched operations than any other – repeatedly described a damaging 'targets culture'. It concluded that: 'The Director of Operations gave an impression of having focused on individual tasks, such as the achieving of targets, at the expense of leading the overall operation of the Trust.'[53]

The very narrow conception of public servants' motivations expressed in targets and incentives policies often failed to improve efficiency and empower people. Instead, public employees who had historically enjoyed a great deal of autonomy and responsibility were reduced to satisfying narrow objectives in order to increase their wages. And there's a big problem with this. Those public officials, robbed of their true responsibilities, are no longer able to take account of the future in the course of their jobs. They've been reduced to taking short-term stop-gap approaches to serious long-term problems.

Perhaps this wouldn't have mattered so much had those politicians in Whitehall – now more powerful than ever – been able to take account of the long term in their own decision-making. But, at the very moment those public-sector professionals had their responsibilities taken away, politicians themselves decided to put the future to one side.

How individualism changed elections

As with the reform of public services, the reason this happened is intrinsically related to the insights of public-choice theorists. This time, however, the changes would cut right to the heart of the notion of what a political party is, and even how our democracy should work.

By the 1990s, the dogma that citizens should, as much as possible, be treated like individual consumers by government was already embedded in public-sector management techniques. But it had also been written deep into society, not so much as a result of these reforms as of the massive consumer boom fuelled by the rise of lifestyle marketing that had been developed in the 1970s. Against this backdrop Britain's Labour party, wedded to socialist ideas of redistribution, nationalisation and government control, feared they would be out of power for good. By 1992 the Labour party had suffered four successive election defeats.

To regain power, a small group of Labour 'modernisers'[54] focused around Peter Mandelson, the party's head of communications, began to consider what it would really take for Labour to win an election.[55] In particular, one member of the group called Philip Gould, a strategy and polling advisor, perceived that a growing section of British voters weren't doing what political analysts might traditionally have expected them to do. While they had broadly accepted the terms of the Thatcher era, supporting low taxes, a smaller state and the rise of consumerism, they were no longer certain Conservative supporters. To win again, Gould realised, Labour must ruthlessly pursue them. He later called it 'the heart of the 1997 election strategy', and he did it by running weekly and sometimes daily focus groups with Conservative swing voters, not only to discover what policies they might support but to understand their psychology – their lifestyles and values – using techniques of modern market research that had originated in the 1970s to sell products to the self-expressive baby boomers.[56] Gould had seen this method in action before, on frequent trips to the Clinton election and re-election campaigns in the US, used by pollster Dick Morris, who has explained what he sought to do for the president:

> 'I felt that the most important thing for [Bill Clinton] to do was to bring to the political system the same consumer rules/philosophy that the business community has. Because politics needs to be as responsive to the whims and the desires of the marketplace as business is, and it needs to be as sensitive to the bottom line – profits or votes – as a business is.'[57]

Gould used a second mechanism to ensure that the positions New Labour took would appeal to voters. The Morris Concept of Triangulation, named after its creator, Dick Morris, was designed to 'create a third position, not just in between the old positions of the two parties but above them as well'.[58]

Using this technique, Gould could ensure that Tony Blair, as Labour leader, would always occupy the central ground of politics, even if that meant that his policies seemed to diverge from those of his own party, because this would force his opponents to take extreme positions. It was a ruthless strategy for winning elections.

Throughout the history of the Labour movement there had been a tension between pollsters, who felt that the party's objective was simply to win, and politicians, who felt it was their job to convince voters that their policies and views were worth electing. It was a debate first played out between Mark Abrams, the author of *The Teenage Consumer* who worked as Labour's original private pollster, and Labour MPs like Richard Crossman in the 1960s. Crossman issued a withering response to Abrams's determination to give people what they wanted. 'Those who assert that their sole object should be to regain office', wrote Crossman, 'seem to me to misconceive not merely the nature of British socialism, but the working of British democracy.'[59] For years Crossman's assumptions held sway, and they found their logical conclusion in the 1983 Labour manifesto, dubbed 'the longest suicide note in history' by Gerald Kaufman MP. The party campaigned on a prospectus that gave no quarter to populism, and as a result Labour suffered their worst-ever election defeat. Much of the motivation behind Gould and the Labour modernisers' reforms was to stop this from happening again. They realised that by tailoring policy to people's individual desires they could ensure that Labour would take and hold power.

You get a sense of this from the personal pledges made by Tony Blair to the electorate in 1997, which included guarantees that Labour would 'cut class sizes to 30 or under for five-, six- and seven-year-olds' and 'fast-track punishment for persistent young offenders', and a commitment to keep 'interest rates as low as possible'. There were no values linking these different pledges, there was no ideological critique or vision of society at work, only piecemeal responses to the focus groups.

But Gould's victory represented more than simply the success of a particular election-winning tactic; it was an entirely different vision of democracy. Crossman, and almost all of his contemporaries on the left and right, believed in representative democracy in which those who stood for office were expected to state honestly and explicitly what they believed and intended to do once elected. In this way, voters could rationally and objectively weigh up what direction the country should travel in and vote accordingly. Gould believed that this was inefficient and, worse, elitist. He argued that if Labour was to represent modern Britain, Crossman's version of politics had to be abandoned: 'For a time,' he wrote later, 'Labour forgot about suburban voters, and it was only when the party was able to connect with the fears and aspirations of these ordinary, hard-working families – to become genuinely a party of the people once more – that it could form a government.'[60] People would be treated like consumers not only when they visited a hospital or got on a train, but also at the ballot box. Even after that, when Labour had been elected, Gould continued to run focus groups that would help find 'dividing lines' between mainstream public opinion and opposition policies. He called it 'the new politics – leading and listening, accessibility and accountability'.[61] But what actually happened was rather different. By constantly responding to the whim of focus groups and taking bold new and often incongruous positions, Britain's political parties were forced to sacrifice their ability to formulate long-term policies. The 'new politics' was the politics of now.

Since 1997 a clutch of the senior members of the New Labour project have come forward to admit that Labour's decisions were increasingly erratic and short-term. At the root of these problems, according to Derek Draper, was Gould's 'new politics'. Draper, who once worked as an advisor to Peter Mandelson, recorded an interview during Labour's second term with the documentary-maker Adam Curtis, in which he laid it all out: 'People are contradictory and irrational and so you have a problem in terms of deciding what you're going to do if all you're doing is listening to a mass of individual opinions that are forever fluctuating, don't really have any coherence and, crucially, are not set in context. And that's why people can say, I want lower taxes and better public services. Of course they do. You say, do you want to pay more taxes to get better public services, people are less sure. They then don't believe that if they do pay more taxes, they will be spent on better public services. So you end up in the quagmire.' [62]

Perhaps the most explicit statement of how Labour's 'new politics' ignored the future appears in the book *Good and Bad Power* written by Geoff Mulgan CBE, who worked as the director of the Downing Street Strategy Unit and as head of policy for Tony Blair: 'When I joined the British government in 1997, these pressures [of day-to-day business] had become so intense that the future had effectively been put on hold. Public capital spending had been sharply cut back; budgets were managed year to year; investment in preventing crime or disease had been squeezed. The nearer one came to the centre of power in the mid-1990s the shorter the time horizons were, so that the Prime Minister's closest advisors were rarely looking more than a few weeks or months ahead. Their highest aspiration was simply to survive in power.'[63]

And the effects could be felt, not just in minor areas of domestic policy, but in significant international relationships, which seemed to be decided almost on a whim. Derek Scott, an economics advisor to Tony Blair until 2003, was damning about Labour's approach to the European Union: 'One of the problems for the Blair government has been that in opposition Labour never worked out what being pro-European meant; it was simply part of rebranding and repositioning the party.'[64]

So why did individuals seem to give 'irrational' and incoherent feedback to policy-makers? And why does it always seem to be the case that aggregated individual choices lead to short-termism of the kind that has damaged the prospects of the jilted generation?

Individuals don't always make good decisions

In fact, there's a flaw in one of the most basic assumptions that has informed Britain's political outlook in the last 30 years. Public-choice theorists, neo-liberals and the politicians who followed their ideas all thought that people are best placed to make decisions about their preferences, habits, attitudes, values and tastes. Critical to this view was the idea that people's decisions and preferences don't change over time. As

Nobel Prize-winning economists (and Mont Pelerin members) Gary Becker and George Stigler proclaimed in 1977: 'One does not argue over tastes for the same reason that one does not argue over the Rocky Mountains – both are there, will be there next year, too, and are the same to all men.'[65]

The implication is obvious. Not only do people know what they want today – since likes and dislikes are fixed, they are also best placed to know what's in their future interests as well. Given this, liberal economists argued that those who made choices on behalf of individuals were mistaken.

Becker and Stigler said that people's choices were like mountains – permanent and unchanging over time. They aren't. In the last twenty years, research in many different fields has shown that people's likes and dislikes aren't fixed or stable. They're susceptible to dramatic change.

It's a point that applied scientists have known for years. Back in 1992 Brian Gibbs, a young behavioural scientist working in Chicago University, asked test subjects to rinse their mouths with anti-nail-biting fluid. Half were told that they would be required to do this just once, half that they would repeat the experience twenty times. But when participants were asked to rate their experience after just one taste, those 'who expected to taste the fluid 20 times found it to be less unpleasant than did participants who expected to taste it only once'.[66]

This result was surprising. How could the sensation of bitterness be radically altered by a difference in verbal instructions? Gibbs realised that people seem to act like 'chameleons', fitting their tastes around their future choices,[67] an observation trialled in experiments 'fundamentally at odds with the picture of the consumer suggested by economic theory', he said. 'Rational consumers maximise utility by selecting goods to suit their tastes, not by selecting their tastes to suit goods.'[68]

This is almost the exact opposite of what Becker and Stigler had written twenty years earlier. And since then, other research has revealed that context can change how much people eat and drink. When people own objects, they rate them 'more positively in terms of attractiveness, value and quality of design'.[69] And it has even been shown that if people don't like something, they can be made to consume more of it by subtle changes in environment.[70]

If people's preferences change depending on the setting and their environment, so they can also change over time. Working in the mid-1990s, George Loewenstein, the behavioural economist and great-grandchild of Sigmund Freud, tried to use coffee mugs to get an answer to this question. His subjects, US college students, were first shown a mug and then told that they would be given it in the near future. When they were given it, they would then have the option of selling it back for cash. But before anything was given away, they were asked for the minimum price they'd be willing to sell the mug for. His test subjects weren't very good at the task. As Loewenstein concluded, '[They] underestimated their own selling prices substantially, as if they failed to appreciate the fact that they would become attached to the object once they were endowed with it'.[71]

Other psychologists have found that people regularly make poor estimations of how bad or good they will feel about certain outcomes like the results of an exam, or living with a persistent health problem. People also have a tendency to believe that one factor – like a holiday or a new car – will increase their happiness levels far more than it does. When faced with the outcomes, people often feel far less positive or negative about the experience than they predicted.

As Loewenstein says: 'Healthy people often state that they are not interested in receiving "heroic measures" if they become ill – chemotherapy, life support systems, resuscitation – but sick people are far more interested in receiving such care. Whose preferences should we act on [those who are healthy today, or the sick people they will become]?'[72] Because the axiom of modern British politics contends that individuals' decisions are always correct, it has no serious answer to this question, since it makes no allowance for the idea that people's opinions can change. As Cass Sunstein and Richard Thaler, authors of the bestselling behavioural economics text, *Nudge*, state: 'No one believes individuals make decisions like economists expect them to because people just don't possess complete information, have unlimited cognitive abilities and exercise total self-control.'[73] Yet the entire thrust of the last 30 years of British politics has ignored this – with huge implications.

If, like Thatcher, you believe that individuals will always make the best possible decisions in a free market, it means there's a limit to your beliefs. If, like Major and Blair, you consider that giving more public-sector choice to individuals will always get them better services, that's almost certainly flawed. But if, like Gould, you attempt to decide policy on the basis of what people say they desire in a focus group, you really are doomed in the long term because their opinions will change and your policies will become incoherent. You also turn politics into a technical branch of marketing and politicians into cynical salesmen convinced that citizens are just self-interested customers and that if you just give them what they want, the customer will be happy.[74] But if they don't know what they want, or their opinions change over time and in different circumstances, you can't win.

The limits of this kind of decision-making were eventually found by New Labour after September 11th 2001, when it became increasingly clear to Tony Blair that the defence of British and Western values through foreign policy must take priority over voter preferences. He considered that Britain's interests could be better protected in the long term by him than by public opinion, ignoring the one million-strong march through London against the Iraq war in 2003. One year later, he explained to Labour conference delegates exactly why his vision of leadership had changed.

> 'I don't think as a human being, as a family man, I've changed at all. But I have changed as a leader. I have come to realise that caring in politics isn't really about "caring". It's about doing what you think is right and sticking to it … There has been no third way, this time. Believe me, I've looked for it.'[75]

Blair had realised that Gould's model of democracy didn't always work, that good leadership requires more than popularity: it requires judgement. It doesn't require focus groups leading policy, it requires leaders to put a convincing case to citizens. Though, in the case of Iraq, some say Blair failed on both counts.

Britain's new establishment

But the kind of politics Blair had critiqued by 2004 had already reshaped party politics in Britain. One of William Hague's first acts as leader of the Conservative party in 1997 was to pass around copies of Gould's biography of the Labour campaign: *The Unfinished Revolution*. Soon these ideas were transforming Conservative politics too. As the election guru Professor Dennis Kavanagh explains, the effects on both parties were dramatic: 'The focus in marketing is on target voters, particularly those voters the party needs to capture if it is to win the election; in other words, some voters are more important than others, and, tragically for the activists, marketing regards the task of reassuring the potential converts or potential defectors as a higher priority than appeasing established supporters.'

As a result, parties become increasingly centralised. 'The marketing men prefer a party that is centralised, leader friendly, allows them direct access to the key decision-makers, including the leader, and grants much autonomy to the people they liaise with – usually the party's communication directors. Internal debate should be sacrificed in the interests of presenting a clear message. It should have what Philip

Gould, Blair's polling strategist, calls "a unitary command structure".[76]

In modern British politics both Labour and Conservative parties now have these structures, with the effect that their members have been marginalised. So while 4 per cent of the British population were members of a political party in 1980, just 1 per cent is involved today.[77]

The result of all this is curiously ironic. Blair, Major and Thatcher were all fascinated by the idea of a 'classless' society. Gould believed the very motivation for his polling alchemy was to empower a silent majority of Britain. Thatcher and her advisors were suspicious of the old elites and the powerful, faceless British establishment identified and railed against in the 1960s. And all of these politicians used precisely the same technique to replicate the relationship between business and consumer in government – even using business techniques of market research to get elected in the first place. These mechanisms, however, have centralised state power and hollowed out the political movements that brought them to office. And the result is that Britain is now governed by a new elite, what journalist Peter Oborne calls 'the political class'. Thatcher, Major and Blair have created a much more powerful establishment than the one they sought to destroy. This new establishment is made up not just of politicians but their advisors, lobbyists and journalists; and their relationships cut across party lines and political fences and are as entrenched and familial as any Baroque court.

In the Labour party, this political class is exemplified by the former ministers Ed Balls and Yvette Cooper, who are married, and Ed Miliband and David Miliband, who are brothers. Even Philip Gould, now Lord Gould, has watched with pride while senior Labour figures like Tessa Jowell and Alastair Campbell attempted to support his 22-year-old daughter's attempts to win a safe Labour seat at the 2010 election.[78] Britain's new coalition also has some very old faces. The Liberal Democrat leader, Nick Clegg, has a new special advisor called Richard Reeves who used to work for the New Labour government under pensions minister Frank Field. For some, membership of the political class is much more important for those in its number than any petty party affiliation.[79] And what better evidence is there of the triumph of the political class than the fact that British politics, more centralised than ever before, is also led by the second man in succession who has failed to win a general election?

One reason for this is that all three political parties are increasingly similar, since the competition to occupy the centre ground of politics has only increased. In 1997, Gould was desperate to ensure that Labour won the support of that growing group of floating voters. In the 2010 election the group had grown again, and now all three parties were desperately fighting to win their support. And they all used precisely the same techniques that Gould championed in the 20th century, moving far from their traditional positions in the hope of winning votes.

This, finally, provides an explanation of why Britain's politicians failed to honestly debate the national deficit before the election. Both Labour and the Conservatives were attempting to position themselves in the middle ground of British politics, both were finding a totally spurious 'dividing line' of just £6bn in cuts; and if their stated positions weren't exactly triangulated, they were certainly not the genuine positions of either party. With both fatally compromised in this way, neither one of the leaders was prepared to reveal the truth. And that seems to be a much more powerful example of politicians' 'contempt' for the public than the word 'bigoted' used to describe Gillian Duffy.

This isn't the logical conclusion of Philip Gould's political strategising. To suggest that it is dramatically overstates his role and dramatically underestimates everything else that happened. Looking back on the last 50 years of British politics, it almost seems as if his strategies, the techniques he learned from Dick Morris, were the inevitable political consequence of the rise of the individual and the consumer class.

After all, if business was so successful at giving people what they want in the marketplace, why shouldn't this be celebrated? And if the mechanisms of the free market can work for the purchase of 'a particular music system or your clothing', as Yankelovich said, why couldn't those mechanisms work to provide you with education or local government or housing? And if people still aren't getting what they want, why not liberalise further, give them more choice, give doctors and teachers more incentives, more targets? 'Don't want the carrot? Too bad, here's the stick.' Because people must be efficient, because you can incentivise marriage as if stable relationships and children and a happy home aren't what people want anyway. 'Well, perhaps they're not', said our politicians. 'Who are we to judge? All we can do, in fact, is release the new consumers from the horrifying oppression of the society we inherited.'

So they set us free, with our 'complete information, unlimited cognitive abilities and total self-control', and it slowly dawned on them that we don't always have these. That we are, in fact, human after all.

In a quest for 'classlessness', society's divisions have only been entrenched; following the fight for 'individuals', state controls have only been centralised; and after ridding Britain of its vicious 'establishment', we've been given another more powerful elite barely able to serve the jilted generation, and who seem unable to commit to, or admit to, the future. So perhaps it's time to say we've had enough, that our politics can thrive only when there are honest debates about the issues that shape our society. Perhaps, just perhaps, we actually want our future back.

We don't blame our parents' generation for this. Just because they're all individuals doesn't mean that they're frenzied individualists too. We begrudge them neither their wealth nor their freedom. Many, many good things have happened. But the slice-by-slicing away of the language of the future has created serious problems in this country. It sometimes feels like we're led by those who say that the language of the future isn't theirs, that discussing 'ideals' or 'ideology' or 'what is right' is a dangerous thing. That way, they warn, lie the communists and the fascists of the 20th century – driving their peoples on a mad, lethal and endless quest towards Utopia. But, of course, what they forget to mention is that those same dangerous ideas of a better future also fought communism, fought fascism and built civilisation.

The long march to democracy wasn't founded on the individual, or on the desire to destroy government, but by increasing the accountability of the decisions made on our behalf. We know these collective decisions aren't perfect; they don't deliver what everyone wants all of the time, or even some of the time. Politics is compromise.

Times are tough. Complex long-term problems surround us. So, it will not be sufficient in the coming years for a tiny band of politicians to cede an infinity of choices to us and assume their work is done. Government is required to do more than simply provide people with options. When this is forgotten, the decisions taken can be short-term and that can do huge unintended damage. It's a lesson our generation is learning the hard way, in our agency jobs and our shorthold flats, with our mounting debts and stumbling lives lived far away from the high tables of populist politics. We know that our parents didn't want it this way; we know that when they accepted the terms of their society they were only trying to do what was best for themselves and their families. But we also now know that they could have done better if more of them had remembered that they aren't just individuals but citizens too.

CONCLUSION

The most deplorable thing about the government continuing to land students with more and more debt is that they got their education free. They'll do fine for pensions, they have little debt and have made a fortune in property by buying it when they were our age. What will our generation get? Ten years of paying off debts, a laughable pension that'll be worth less than we pay in and the prospect of paying extortionate rents to the very generation who lucked out. We are the jilted generation and one day we'll all realise it and do something about it.

Ben Morgan, BBC News website, reader comments, 1 December 2003

We only discovered this quote from a BBC message board months into researching this book, and we didn't manage to track down Ben Morgan,[1] but back in 2003 he seemed to express much of what this book is about. He wasn't the first, nor the last, to realise our generation's predicament. In 2010 members of the jilted generation enjoyed not a 'Summer of Love' but a 'Summer of Discontent'[2] in which new graduates entered an employment market where 69 applicants were chasing every job – twice as many as during the 1982 recession. Today, some employers are openly admitting that they reject on sight any application from a graduate with a 2:2 or less. These are unprecedented numbers, but they don't really explain what's going on. In part, this book has been an attempt to do that – to unravel the consequences of a tough jobs market and big debts for young people – and this, very briefly, is what we already know:

In 2010 Britain's graduates left university with an average debt of £17,500, many have failed to get a job, and some have already started drawing welfare payments – and a good proportion of them will continue to do this for the foreseeable future. 2009 was fractionally better, 2011 may be worse. But these guys are the lucky ones. Many more, about half the population in fact, are leaving state schools much earlier, without a place at university, without A-levels; half are leaving without five good GCSEs.[3] A higher proportion of these people will go on benefits and, as things stand, thousands of them will stay on those benefits for the rest of their lives.

Of those who attain legal adulthood and find work, most will also find their wages to be significantly less than they expected, and those who have graduated will find it difficult to pay off their debt. Meanwhile, the number of young entrepreneurs will continue to fall.[4] Almost all will find it impossible to get stable accommodation in which to begin their adult lives – council waiting lists are too long, shorthold tenancy provides little stability – and it will be impossible for all but the most wealthy and successful to get mortgages since, with such poor pay and such heavy debts, no bank will give them a second glance. Computer says no. We might expect that the number of young adults who live at home will rise. There, they will find it difficult to begin and maintain long-term relationships, and some young men will even become more violent as a result.

For all of these people, their journey to genuine adulthood will be put on indefinite hold – until they get a job, or a better-paid and permanent job, until they get a stable home and a relationship, until they can start to meaningfully develop the 'narrative of identity' about which the sociologist Richard Sennett has written so powerfully.

While the circumstances of those young people making their first steps into the adult world of work are peculiarly difficult today, and have been made harder by Britain's harsh economic times, domestic recession and the global downturn don't explain them entirely. Insecure and expensive housing didn't happen overnight but because of a consistent failure to build enough homes. Jobs are more difficult to come by because the traditional mechanisms for 'upskilling' the workforce – formal and informal apprenticeships – have been cut away. Unemployment has been rising among the jilted generation since 2005. Our economic growth has faltered, many argue, because both Britain's private and public sectors haven't invested as highly as they once did.

Instead, our country has been gripped by the irresistible force of 'now', and the decisions that have been made about the direction we should take have been depressingly short-term. A vision of individual 'rights' and self-expressive choices has taken hold of our politics and shaped our society. This has led us to imagine that personal inheritance is more important than societal inheritance. (In raw financial terms, this is incorrect: even after Britain's young people eventually inherit, they will still be £33,000 worse off than their parents, as we saw in Chapter 3.) It has led us to assume that doing the best for ourselves will always be best for others, but this is demonstrably untrue. And this individualistic vision has utterly seduced our politicians, who seem convinced that democratic decisions will always be inferior to the ones we make alone, forgetting almost entirely that the reason we have government in the first place is because some decisions require collective action for the general good. Chief among these are decisions that regard the long term and that shape our nation's future.

It's already clear, however, that many don't see this. At the time of writing, the raising of university tuition fees is under discussion; little has yet been offered to the jobless young; and the chancellor has already committed to cuts in public-sector investment until 2015.

'Rights and responsibilities'

Against this background, Britain's political elite seems to have little to offer the jilted generation but sound-bites. Young people have been labelled as 'Kippers', 'Neets', 'iPods' and 'Boomerang Kids' and they have been lectured almost constantly about 'responsibility' by politicians. Tony Blair coined the threadbare phrase 'rights and responsibilities' more than a decade ago and the jargon has been used by every political leader since. All of them, at one time or another, have applied it to young people; they have said that if the jilted generation just took some more accountability for themselves, stopped being anti-social and so short-term, things would work out okay. There's no defence for anti-social behaviour but, as ever, things are more complicated than they are presented to be. And if an entire generation of people are growing up only to find that they have no access to the jobs and homes with which they will build their adult lives, it's not a big surprise, surely, that they fail to 'take responsibility'.

Worse, politicians themselves are short-term. They too can be irresponsible. They too often fail to take responsibility, even choosing to hide their decisions from the public. So perhaps there's a problem with the language of 'rights and responsibilities'. It was designed by Blair to be a sort of catch-all term for what being a citizen, or transacting more generally with the state, should look like: 'You have a right to vote, you have a responsibility to pay taxes'; 'You have a right to privacy from the state, you have a responsibility to obey the law'; 'You have a right to claim expenses, you have a responsibility not to use those expenses to buy a duck house, or a flat screen, or your adult channel subscription'.[5] However, the phrase 'rights and responsibilities' doesn't speak meaningfully to employment problems or housing problems; it doesn't speak to national debts and personal ones. And it doesn't address, therefore, the most fundamental problems that face our 'irresponsible' generation. 'Rights' are fixed; 'human rights', we're told, are designed to be timeless (though they seem to be subject to quite remarkable change) and the 'responsibilities' associated with them are also fixed: voters should always pay taxes, taxpayers should always get a vote. The same isn't true, however, of jobs or housing or public healthcare or education. These aren't fixed concepts. No one, however much politicians claim otherwise, actually has a 'right' to a job, or a 'right' to affordable housing. And we know this because the jilted generation don't have the same job and housing prospects as their parents did – ours are worse. If these things really were 'rights', we could say that our 'rights' have been diminished. But a job has to be earned. Housing can be paid for by individuals or the state, and how much we pay is subject to massive change. So perhaps, nearly twenty years after 'rights and responsibilities' became the lingua franca of British politics, it has outstayed its welcome. It's time to let it go.

Benefits and obligations

We need some new words, and some new thinking that refers not to 'rights' but to the practical issues that matter to us; an approach that's not short-term and myopic, but that will restore the proper functions of politics by placing the future at the heart of our democracy. This is a point that the Scottish philosopher David Hume drew out in his *Treatise of Human Nature* (1739–40), in which he warned about short-term thinking. 'There is no quality in human nature', he wrote, 'which causes more fatal errors in our conduct, than that which leads us to prefer whatever is present to the distant and remote, and makes us desire objects more according to their situation than their intrinsic value.' And to tackle this, he explained, required understanding that government has two separate functions: the administration of rights, or 'conventions of mutual interest' as he called them; and the seeking of 'advantage' through 'common purpose'.[6]

For Hume, government becomes 'one of the finest and most subtle inventions imaginable' when it works towards this common purpose;[7] and if we want 'fine and subtle' government rather than rough and blundering government, it's imperative that we stop obsessing about 'whatever is present' and reawaken our sense of ourselves relative to times past and future.

If the idea of 'rights and responsibilities' can't help us to do this, a notion of 'benefits and obligations' can. We should talk of 'benefits' because pensions, education, healthcare, investment and the economy are all, unlike 'rights', flexible and subject to change. They are gifts given by those at work before us. And we should talk of 'obligations' because, just as these things are all given to us freely – merely for being born in Britain in this time – we have an implicit obligation to pass them on to the next generation.

Benefits and obligations aren't new ideas, but they tend not to be codified or explicit. They are already essential characteristics in our own lives: each of us receives the benefit of being raised by parents or guardians and has an obligation, if we have children, to raise them too. We perhaps also have an obligation to care for our own parents and family in the event that they need it. It's a transfer of good-will, to ensure the continued success of our families and relationships. To extend the idea to the country ensures the continued success of our society. That's not an original idea, just one that has been recently set aside.

Casting back to 1979, the year of birth for the oldest members of the jilted generation, you can get a sense of how this change in approach would have ameliorated some of the greatest problems we now face. Examine, for example, Margaret Thatcher's victory speech of that year in which she said: 'By bringing in legislation which will give to every council tenant the right to buy his own home at a substantial discount and with a 100 per cent mortgage, we will start to transform the housing picture.'[8]

There was no 'right' to buy council property as Thatcher described it: the opportunity was limited to one particular group of people – council tenants – at one particular time – the 1980s. There's no comparable 'right' for our generation today because most of the homes have been sold and Britain now faces an acute shortage of council accommodation. But there was also no 'right' to buy because council housing is not a 'right' but a 'benefit', created by earlier governments and generations who had sought to address an acute social need. A 'benefit' had been made available to Thatcher's tenants and the implicit 'obligation' that came with that benefit – to address housing needs by replacing the stock and investing the receipts from housing sales – was ignored. And now we have a desperate housing crisis because every subsequent government has ignored it too.

Or take Tony Blair's speech to Labour supporters at the Royal Festival Hall on the morning of 2 May 1997, in which

he said: 'Today we have set objectives for a new Labour government: a world-class education system, in which education
is not the privilege of the few but the right of the many in our
country.'[9]

Further education (to which he was referring)[10] is not a
'right' – you can't codify it in law – and certainly not when
nearly half the population are leaving school without five
decent GCSEs. Had Blair not considered education a 'right' –
which simply had to be fulfilled regardless of who paid and at
what cost – but a 'benefit' that he enjoyed free with the associated obligation to provide it and, in a knowledge economy,
even improve on it in the future; if Blair had examined his
student loans and tuition fees in this context, perhaps they
might never have come about? At this distance it's impossible
to say.

The neutral state

What we can say is that the very narrow conception of
what an individual is, that 'utility-maximising rational actor'
invented by economists and public-choice theorists, would
support Blair's decisions. After all, if you're self-interested,
and benefits have been bestowed on you by previous generations, why on earth would you, acting rationally, seek to
pass them on to others whom you don't know and will never
meet? You would not, since to do so would necessarily limit
your 'utility'. Just as further education is now paid for by the
graduates who receive it, so successive governments acting
on behalf of these 'utility-maximisers' have worked to absorb
and spend benefits that shouldn't apply only to them but

to future generations too – be they public utilities or North Sea oil. Worse, they have even put the cost of their current spending onto future generations through high public debt and PFI schemes. Shorn of any serious sense of obligation to the future, their focus instead has been to attempt to be neutral – making no moral judgement about the present and acknowledging no legacy from the past. The previous chapter described some of the problems that have emerged as a result of the move towards this kind of state, but to really understand how flawed this perspective is, let's undertake a quick thought-experiment.

Imagine the future of the jilted generation under the purest conception of the 'neutral state'. A world of individuals liberated to make any choice and granted absolute freedoms. As rational actors, aware of the information contained within this book – the lack of prospects in the jobs market, the lack of decent housing, the public and private debts, the lack of investment – what would induce the young to stay in this country? The answer for the young rational actor is to depart these shores. The most economically rational thing would be for all 13 million of us to pack our bags and move to where the environment is better suited to our ends – where our taxes wouldn't be spent paying off another generation's debt, and where the actions of the society had well prepared the building-blocks for our future – a country like Sweden or Norway.

Imagine then, if that happened, what would become of the 'young' country that Blair so enthusiastically celebrated. When the last of us had finally waved goodbye at the dock-side or the check-in gate, how would our parents' generation survive? Who would pay their pensions? Who would cover their buy-to-let rents? Where would they get their interns from? How would the national debt be paid? The country would surely sink into a ruin.

Actually, in the era of globalisation it's very possible that migrants from poorer parts of the world would – perhaps eagerly – fill our shoes. It's all very simple. Labour and talent go to where they are most efficiently employed. Youth from Africa, South East Asia, Eastern Europe and the Indian subcontinent could travel to Britain to plug the gap and take up the slack. They would suffer these pains only because the prospects in their own countries are bad enough to motivate them to leave. And so the world becomes a merry-go-round of migration. People move to where they are most productive, communities break down and eventually societies and nations with them. The 'neutral state' would take no interest in defending them: it can't pay any heed to the idea of benefits and obligations passed down through time, but can only create a disinterested future – in the interest of no one in particular. In this way the 'neutral state' sows the seeds of its own destruction, since it becomes a state without a society, run by a government with no constituency in mind.

Or is it that simple? In the real world the vast proportion of the jilted generation wouldn't move. People are more than just rational economic actors and therefore they are disposed to making their communities work for them. They are tied to where they live by more than just monetary prospects. They are coupled to their societies by a sense of history, culture, and language. They are bonded to their communities through the relationships they have formed. They have roots that cannot be dug up and planted elsewhere without bearing a loss. People don't really act like 'utility-maximisers', so it makes no sense at all to govern on their behalf as if they were.

And, deep down, our politicians also know this. Britain hasn't really been ruled as a 'neutral state' at all. In the era that champions individuals, the state has grown in size and strength and remit, even while those in power have criticised it for being too big. The reason for this is that politicians still recognise that they need to ameliorate social injustice and human hardship and the collapse of community. There are direct political consequences for those who stand for election and ignore them. The trouble is that in an age of 'individualism' the language of the 'neutral state' ends up justifying this very biased – non-neutral – action. And that's precisely why Tony Blair and Margaret Thatcher crowbarred the word 'rights' into their discussion of universities and council houses. They seemed to have no framework but freedom in which to conceive of education and shelter.

End of the neutral state

As soon as politicians restore the language of the future to their lexicon, and think about government in terms of benefits and obligations, they will quickly find that the state can no longer be neutral, and they will be free to talk honestly about the problems that really matter to people. No longer, either, will it be acceptable for them to pretend that the tough decisions they face can be foisted onto individuals.

Some decisions have to be taken collectively. Take the funding of state pensions: this issue cannot be settled equitably by pensioners. It will require central government to take a view and enforce a policy, but the consequences of that policy will have to be justified in terms of the future. Some politicians will believe it should be moral for pension payments to rise, others will disagree, but one thing they can't continue to do is leave the problem to the long term. So if the current generation of politicians want the benefit of comfortable retirement funded by a decent pension, then they are obligated to ensure that the system can be sustainable for future generations to enjoy too. It can't just be a cheap trick from which one generation gains a special advantage, nor can they continue to ignore the inevitable. And here's the truth – politicians can create a sustainable pensions policy only if they have also taken a robust view about what kind of society they want. This kind of debate would be much more honest than simply pushing the issue to one side as others have done. One thing is certain: in a debate about the future, politicians are unlikely to all sound the same.

Nor does the idea of benefits and obligations imply that power must be centralised. In fact, since a politics that conceives of the future will be inherently more partial and less focused on easy plays for the centre-ground, central government must be careful to exercise its judgements delicately; the problems of a centralised state future-proofing its society are well expressed by the insanities of Stalinist Russia, for example. In fact, much damage has been done to the future prospects of the jilted generation precisely because communities have been shut out of deciding their futures. So a forward-looking government must also be decentralised, transparent and responsive.

Generally speaking, the closer people are to the power that's exercised on their behalf, the better that power will be administered in a democracy. For this reason, the decisions by the coalition government to channel power to local communities – through the election of police chiefs and more local referendums – are very welcome; so too are undertakings to ensure greater transparency at all levels of government. It's impossible to be an active citizen if the information that relates to the governance of your society is hidden from you. But these systemic reforms must go further. Indeed, they won't go very far at all if the attitude of government remains fundamentally suspicious of decisions that communities make for themselves, and if local politics also sets aside the future.

Implementing benefits and obligations

Government on behalf of individuals makes a fetish of freedom and 'rights' and obsesses about a very specific system to provide those rights, namely, the free market. This often doesn't work very well, because there are simply too many things that government, whether local or national, has to do that don't concern 'freedoms' at all, and not surprisingly the free market can't help. Perhaps the most potent example of how this flawed thinking has hurt the jilted generation concerns our housing.

In Chapter 1, the story of how Britain's developers were given carte blanche to provide housing in a free market ended with fewer homes than we needed and prices too high for our generation. In the last decade, 93 per cent of the homes built in London have been poky one- and two-bedroom flats. These aren't the homes our generation needs; they're not built to raise families in, but have been designed to appeal to speculators who believe that they can turn a profit by renting them out.

In this way the free market has failed to provide us with the affordable, stable homes enjoyed by previous generations – the benefit – and, as a result, the obligation to our generation has not been met. The system itself has taken priority over the human beings the system claims to serve. To put this right doesn't require an abandoning of freedoms, it doesn't require a denial of rights – instead it requires a conception of the future. So, the first question we need to settle is: in an ideal world, what would Britain's housing supply look like? This isn't difficult to work out. We have a housing crisis because we have too few, too small and too poorly-made homes, and those that exist offer little stability at high cost for the shorthold tenant.

So, first, we should get shorthold tenancy agreements right. These contracts can, and should, be set for any length of time that the landlord and tenant see fit, but since the default standard contract offered to tenants is for six months, the legal protection tenants have over their homes is necessarily limited. By simply switching the default up to twelve or eighteen months, many tenants would automatically gain more legal protection. A simple switch like this would improve stability for many young tenants. However, it wouldn't address prices. To do that we need more development, increasing the supply of homes to rent and buy.

One way to increase development – the pre-free-market plan – would be for government to simply requisition a vast amount of land and build suitable housing. 'Strategic planning' of this kind has been tried by governments who have attempted to use large swaths of suburban public land to build 'eco-towns'. However, most of the recent schemes have failed to come to fruition. Furthermore, the idea of creating centralised concrete crime hotspots, of the kind built by some local authorities in the 1960s and 70s, is not desirable.

What may be worth considering, however, is the reintroduction of a basic mandatory framework for new development, imposing minimum room sizes and building standards. Since the supply of homes is currently so short, the competitive forces of the free market don't function to maintain quality, and so developers can build small properties to a very low standard. People are so desperate for a home that developers can get away with building and selling almost anything. This isn't in anyone's interest save their shareholders. So, if only to protect future residents, Britain should be reconsidering the expansion of a new Parker Morris standard for homes.[11]

Next, the developers' response to this legislation may be to say that it's unworkable, that the costs will be too great upon their businesses. Though the hundreds of millions of pounds of profits they made before the recession tell another story, developers should be reminded that society maintains a whip hand over them. Why? Because they can't build without our permission. The very act of granting planning permission confers massive profit on a development site before a single shovel of earth is moved, so some basic standards are a small price to pay – indeed too small a price. 'Planning gain' – the increase in land value derived from planning permission – must be used more effectively by public authorities who represent us. In the last ten years, the government seems to have almost completely forgotten the power they hold on our behalf. In the past, a proportion of this planning gain has been taken from developers by the state in exchange for consent. Under Labour, this refund was gradually reduced by central government as an incentive to get private builders working. The trouble is, it hasn't worked. Even before the recession ground housing development to a halt, building rates in the UK were at an all-time low.

So how many homes are missing? Using the same measurements and statistics that appear in Chapter 1, it's possible to calculate that Britain has built 1.44 million fewer homes in the last eleven years compared to the average house-building rates between 1951 and 1980. So, excluding land costs, we estimate that the price of building enough to satisfy this housing shortfall is some £51.8 billion in today's money.[12] While that's not a lot – even £5 billion each year for a decade would cover most of the costs – in the new era of 'austerity Britain', it seems unlikely that there will be sufficient political will to invest the money. We believe local and central government should make house-building a higher priority, but without more public funding there are limited options: it certainly won't be sufficient to hope that things improve and the market will come good, since house prices are falling again and the builders seem little motivated to build. Instead, we could always build the new homes ourselves.

This is exactly what the community group London Citizens is doing, by taking not-for-profit land trust models that exist in Sweden and Vermont, USA, which buy and then protect land in order to provide affordable housing for local communities. They have set up a Community Land Trust (CLT) designed to protect the land by promising never to sell it. The CLT then builds affordably-priced homes which it sells specifically to local families. The land remains the property of the local community, so when families buy the homes they pay just a fraction of the price.

In a sense the scheme is the exact opposite of Thatcher's right to buy scheme. Because the land is held in a permanent trust, the subsidy doesn't just apply to one group of people at one time, but to everyone who lives in the homes for all time. And anyone in London can become a member of the Trust and apply for the housing through London Citizens for just £10.[13]

Just as there are groups of citizens working to transform their communities' housing prospects, so too there are groups that seek to change the relationship between workers and their firms. The Employee Ownership Association (EOA), whose members include John Lewis and the multinational engineering firm Arup (which built the London 2012 Olympic Stadium), assists employees with the knowledge and acumen they need to buy their firms. The EOA wants to see companies running businesses on behalf of their workers. John

Lewis describes its core philosophy as 'labour employing capital, not capital employing labour'.

And these aren't just pipe-dreams. Employee-owned companies currently contribute some £25bn to the British economy. They out-perform the FTSE by roughly 10 per cent each year.[14] Crucially, they also create jobs more quickly than private firms and have been significantly more resilient in an economic downturn.[15]

Today, there are ways of financing businesses of this kind. The Baxi Partnership Trust, for example, will provide up to £2 million in funds for trusts. The Trust began when Philip Baxendale and his cousin sold their boiler-manufacturing company for a tenth of its value to its employees. In 2000 they put £20 million into a fund that they have been using to lend to other employees who might want to do the same. Their three principles for lending aim to ensure that the businesses they help continue for ever to be employee-owned, to be professionally managed, and always to have regard to the interests of their employees.

Similarly, when the credit crunch hit, a group of East Anglian businessmen led by an entrepreneur called Nigel Brown decided to develop the 'Cambridge Boring Bank', designed to channel private investment into the local economy. Brown believes this localised investment can offer better lending rates for borrowers and higher levels of return for investors than large multinationals, and can target investment at a time when larger institutions have been reluctant to do this.

But institutions like these aren't a new thing. Britain's co-operative movement dates back to the 18th century in Scotland, and the 19th in England. It was created so that workers could afford products they couldn't purchase on their own. The first successful co-operative enterprise began in Rochdale – not far from where Gordon Brown would face humiliation at the hands of a pensioner and a live microphone. More recently, the Co-operative Group has developed into supermarkets, shops and even banking. The idea is simple: all their customers – literally anyone with a membership swipecard – take a share of the profits. In 2009 they doled out £50 million.

What all these movements have in common is that they feature citizens setting aside their personal interests for collective advantage in the long term. The actions of those involved are dictated neither by the state nor by the logic of the public-choice theorists. And if movements like these are replicated and nurtured, they will flourish. There are even signs that they might. The Conservatives in the coalition government have promoted a vision of a 'Big Society' focused around communities and empowered citizens, and there are campaigning groups on the left wing of politics, like Compass, that value and champion the Labour movement's traditions of civic action and engagement.

These movements are laudable not least because there's no better way to ensure that our politics considers the future than by creating long-standing institutions in society that demand it. But this won't solve the problems of unemployment and instability faced by the jilted generation today.

As we showed in the last chapter, the specific circumstances we face didn't occur overnight. They were the manifestation of an experiment in social organisation that took decades to mature. Given these unsustainable outcomes, we believe it didn't work. Without a dramatic reappraisal of how we spend both public and private money now, the consequences for young people will be severe. So government, the largest and most legitimate public institution, must act. How it acts – through the restoration of tax breaks for private investment; through the restoration of student grants, even by cutting costs and creating two-year degrees or work-placements that run concurrently with further education courses; through a massive rebuilding of formal apprenticeships; or through a dramatic reinvestment in public housing – should be a matter of open, democratic debate. But things cannot continue as they have done. The authors of this book are not policy-makers; we simply insist that the terms of that debate do not confine themselves only to the present.

The wrong book

People tend to divide post-war British history into two distinct phases: the post-1945 welfare era, and the post-1979 neo-liberal era. Both were 'paradigm shifts' in that the received wisdom of what a government should do, and how, were reconceived.

In 1945, the Attlee government cast the huge resources of a nation united by the war effort against the deepest problems of its people – want, disease, ignorance, squalor, and idleness – the five giants identified by the economist William

Beveridge. These problems would be ameliorated through 'co-operation between the state and the individual' and by a vast and centralised welfare state established to pay for them.

In 1979, the Thatcher government perceived that this co-operation had broken down, that the state was too powerful and that individuals' ambitions, creativity, and self-expression were being thwarted by government. Furthermore, she believed that the future of society could be best advanced by the free market, not the state.

Attlee's reforms were explicitly paternalistic; they were contingent on the vast levers of economic and departmental power located in Whitehall being heaved against the ills of society. Thatcher's reforms were explicitly populist, and stemmed from a deep belief in the power of individuals to shape their own society.

Both reforms were impressive in their scope and success. Attlee transformed a nation ravaged by war, torn by seemingly insurmountable differences in education, class and life expectancy, and gave even the poorest within it genuine prospects. Then Britain was saved again, this time by Thatcher, from a spiralling economic tumult of unproductive industry. She led a renaissance in entrepreneurship. What's more, successive generations in British society have fought to protect the rights of people regardless of their gender or race or sexuality. Minds have been opened, wealth has been created; those iniquitous social barriers that limit the potential of our citizens have been shaken from their foundations. Meanwhile, radical technical innovations have transformed our world and extended the choices we can make about how we live. The jilted generation have much to be thankful for. And we are.

But it has been all too easy to say that the hard work has been done, that history itself has ended, that contrary to New Labour's opening theme, 'things really can't get any better'. We're not buying it. In fact, in the light of a global recession, an unprecedented deficit and increasing social and generational dislocation, fewer and fewer people *are* buying – either the goods and services that power our economy or the ideas of individualism that some claim are the only basis on which to run our society.

We hope it's clear from this book that we believe in capitalism, we believe that the mechanisms of the market are appropriate; that the creation of wealth is not just desirable but vital – it's the underpinning of any decision that we take as individuals or as a society. Capitalism should be celebrated, championed and defended, but it should not become fixated upon. And we believe in 'rights'. We believe in the rule of law, the protection of human dignity and security, and the maintenance of contracts through the justice system. But the administration of 'rights', even in the era of the individual, is not the only appropriate prism through which to seek the legitimacy of government action. As complete people there are other mechanisms we use to express ourselves; our concerns can stretch far beyond the acquiring and maintaining of material wealth or the maintenance of our 'rights' in law. We need security. We need stability and opportunity.

To obtain these things Attlee sought 'co-operation between the state and the individual'; Thatcher saw that relationship as fundamentally antagonistic. We take a different approach. As long as we see the state and the individual as two separate and alien entities in a relationship of increasing or decreasing co-operation, we can never address the problems of the future. Individuals created institutions like the state – but not only the state – to tackle this problem, recognising that shared decisions were often better at preparing for the future than those made by individuals. However, this mechanism has broken down as a result of the centralising of state power and a particular ideology that viewed these group decisions with disdain. We should not abandon our freedoms and autonomy but we must begin to believe in the power of shared decisions once more. The way we shape our futures must be more local to allow these shared decisions to be more responsive to communities' needs. And we must create a relationship between the people and their government that is no longer one of client and provider but of person and community.

In the sweat for votes or wealth, what is really required to sustain us all can be swept aside. Bewildering, unresponsive and vast bureaucracies fail us by placing systems and targets before individuals, by elevating the simple and mechanical above what is fragile and human. There needs to be a deep reappraisal of the language and the ideas that shape our political discourse to reflect the needs of the future – the certain unknown. Our approach to housing, jobs and public resources must once again reflect the needs of our future society and, as we've suggested, it is institutions designed to exist across generations that can make that happen. A simple adjustment of government policy will not ensure that the joblessness and hopelessness, the instability and injustice faced by our generation will be solved for good. It would allow them to declare once again that the hard decisions have been made, that they have won, that history is over.

But history never ends; that's the point. Our problems have not been solved. Too many of the hard decisions have not even been addressed, let alone taken. And all this is bad for us – it's bad for our jilted generation, but it's also bad for those that will follow us, and that's much more important. If Britain's new workers face nearly 70 competitors for every job they apply for, that's a human tragedy. But what if in ten years, in fifteen years, what if at the moment the jilted generation begin to retire, the numbers have stayed the same or got worse? Our interests will not have been protected. Our future will have been abandoned. Our society will expire.

For all these reasons, this book isn't really about us. It's not just about one dissatisfied group in society, a whinge by one generation about another. That would be wrong. This book is about our country's future and our need to safeguard it from those who thought that today was more important than tomorrow; who said that individuals could only succeed alone, who erected grand theories when what we required was simple understanding. For the past three decades every sinew of government has been strained towards the empowerment of individuals and their short-term satisfaction, while the language of politics has made this process seem inexorable. It is not. We continue on this path only while we maintain the fallacy that our desires should be selfish, that we act in isolation or not at all. Don't believe it. You are not alone.

NOTES

Introduction

1. 'Long-term Public Finance Report: An Analysis of Fiscal Sustainability', HM Treasury, 2009, Introduction, p. 4.
2. 'Long-term Public Finance Report: An Analysis of Fiscal Sustainability', HM Treasury, 2002, Introduction, p. 1.
3. Angelique Chrisafis, 'The 1968 crowd had dreams – we are dealing with reality', *Guardian*, 30 March 2006.
4. Richard A. Settersten Jr. and Barbara Ray, 'What's Going on with Young People Today? The Long and Twisting Path to Adulthood', in *Future of Children*, Vol. 20, No. 1, Spring 2010, p. 29.
5. Richard Sennett, *Corrosion of Character: the Personal Consequences of Work in the New Capitalism*, New York: W.W. Norton, 1998, p. 26.
6. Ibid., p. 26.
7. Belinda Turffrey, *The Human Cost*, Shelter, 2010, p. 9.
8. Ibid., p. 13.
9. YouGov poll, March 2010; see *Guardian*: http://www.guardian.co.uk/money/2010/mar/21/house-prices-young-couples-marriage/print
10. Marco Francescone and Katrin Golsch, 'The Process of Globalization and Transitions to Adulthood in Britain', in *Globalization, Uncertainty and Youth in Society*, edited by Hans-Peter Blossfeld, Routledge, 2005, pp. 249–76.
11. David Thomson, *Selfish Generations? How Welfare States Grow Old*, New Zealand: The White Horse Press, 1996, p. 188.

Chapter 1: Housing

1. http://www.guardian.co.uk/politics/2007/may/14/
   uk.labourleadership
2. Lexis Nexis search carried out on 3 April 2010.
3. Hattersley is perhaps speaking from personal experience here
   – he's in his early thirties.
4. http://www.timesonline.co.uk/tol/news/article559752.ece
5. Kenan Malik, *The Moral Maze*, BBC Radio 4, 31 March 2010.
6. Office for National Statistics, *Social Trends*, 40, Chapter 10,
   'Housing', 2009, p. 11.
7. www.cml.org.uk/cml/filegrab/pdf_pub_hf_45-4.pdf.
   pdf?ref=3275
8. Poll: http://www.ipsos-rsl.co.uk/researchpublications/
   researcharchive/poll.aspx?oItemId=526
9. Figures cited in Shelter Press Release, February 2010.
10. Martin Weale, interview with authors, and: http://www.
    guardian.co.uk/business/2007/apr/30/housingmarket.
    houseprices
11. http://www.guardian.co.uk/society/2009/dec/06/right-to-buy-
    housing-thatcher
12. Quoted in Tracy McVeigh, '30 years on, the right to buy
    revolution that still divides Britain's housing estates', *Observer*,
    6 December 2009.
13. For the full story, see Andrew Hosken's *Nothing Like a Dame:
    The Scandals of Shirley Porter* (Granta, 2006).
14. The £85.74bn total figure isn't adjusted for inflation.
    However, according to the HSBC paper, the present valuation
    of the houses sold off is £173.8bn. Another way of calculating
    just part of the intergenerational loss is imagining that the
    government banked the money from each year's sales – not
    including the discount giveaway – into a 5 per cent savings
    account. Today that £45.38bn would be worth £96bn. If there
    had been no discount in the first place, the fund would be
    around double that.

15. Office for National Statistics.

16. http://news.bbc.co.uk/2/hi/uk_news/politics/4287370.stm

17. H. Glennerster and J. Hills (eds), *The State of Welfare: the Economics of Social Spending* (Oxford University Press, 2nd edition, 1998), p. 182.

18. Peter Malpass, 'Housing and the New Welfare State', paper presented at HAS conference, Sheffield Hallam University, April 2004, p. 11.

19. Ibid., p. 9.

20. http://www.guardian.co.uk/politics/2010/jun/13/cuts-threaten-affordable-new-homes

21. Avner Offer, in 'Why has the public sector grown so large in market societies?', *Discussion Papers in Economic and Social History*, No. 44, Oxford University, March 2002.

22. Alan W. Evans, Oliver M. Hartwich, 'Unaffordable Housing: Myths and Fables', Policy Exchange, 2005.

23. Ibid., p. 7.

24. Office for National Statistics, *Social Trends*, 40, Chapter 10, 'Housing', 2009, p. 3.

25. Evans and Hartwich, 'Unaffordable Housing', p. 9.

26. http://www.guardian.co.uk/business/2010/mar/15/first-time-buyers-priced-out

27. *The Arla History of Buy to Let Investment*, 2001–2008, table K, p. 12.

28. http://www.guardian.co.uk/money/2010/apr/12/buy-to-let-first-time-buyers

29. http://www.guardian.co.uk/commentisfree/2010/mar/19/dont-blame-buy-to-let-investors

30. Crisis estimates that there are over 45,000 sofa-surfing young people aged 16–24, another 190,000 who are over 25. See: http://www.crisis.org.uk/policywatch/pages/hidden_homeless.html, March 2010.

31. Family Resources Survey, Department for Work and Pensions, 2008.

32. 'Understanding First Time Buyers', Council of Mortgage Lenders, 2005, p. 41.

33. David Rhodes, 'The Modern Private Rented Sector', Joseph Rowntree Foundation, 2006, p. 44.

34. Office for National Statistics, *Labour Force Survey*, households aged under 30 by tenure.

35. http://www.guardian.co.uk/commentisfree/2010/mar/19/dont-blame-buy-to-let-investors

36. Office for National Statistics, *Social Trends*, 40, Chapter 10, 'Housing', 2009, p. 10.

37. Ibid., p. 7.

38. Quote from Department of Environment, 'Housing: the Government's proposals', White Paper, HMSO, September 1987, as cited in Cathy Sharp, 'Problem Assured: Private renting after the Housing Act 1988', SHAC publications, 1991, p. 24.

39. T. Dodd, 'Private Renting in 1988', HMSO, 1990, and DCLG, 'Rent Lettings and Tenancies', table 731.

40. DCLG, 'Length of Residence by Tenancy', table 802.

41. Belinda Turffrey, *The Human Cost*, Shelter, 2010, p. 14.

42. Ibid., p. 9.

43. Jeremy Coid and Min Yang, 'Violence and Delayed Social Independence Among Young Adult British Men', *Social Psychiatry and Psychiatric Epidemiology*, Vol. 45, No. 3, 2010.

44. Ibid.

45. Liam Reynolds and Nicola Robinson, *Full House? How Overcrowded Housing Affects Families*, Shelter, 2005, p. 19.

46. http://www.guardian.co.uk/money/2010/mar/21/house-prices-young-couples-marriage

47. Turffrey, *The Human Cost*, 2010.

48. http://www.statistics.gov.uk/cci/nugget.asp?id=1921

Chapter 2: Jobs

1.   Michael Portillo, 'Idle young should be entitled to nothing', *Sunday Times*, 30 August 2009.

2.   These figures are taken from the government's unemployment records measured between December 2009 and February 2010. They exclude young people in full-time education.

3.   The Prince's Trust YouGov Youth Index, 2010.

4.   http://www.guardian.co.uk/uk/2010/jan/04/princes-trust-survey-unemployment-young-people

5.   '[There was an increase] in all occupations except Administration and Secretarial; Process, Plant and Machine Operatives; and Elementary Occupations. The largest increase was in Professional Occupations.' Kamran Khan, 'Employment of the older generation', Office for National Statistics, *Economic and Labour Market Review*, Vol. 3, No. 4, April 2009, p. 34.

6.   'Unions Attack Executive Greed As Board Pay Soars', *Independent*, 6 November 2006.

7.   David Willetts, *The Pinch: How the Baby Boomers Stole Their Children's Future and How They Can Give it Back*, London: Atlantic Books, 2009, p. 69.

8.   www.thesun.co.uk/sol/homepage/features/article2409712.ece

9.   http://www.margaretthatcher.org/speeches/displaydocument.asp?docid=111359

10. Ibid.

11. http://www.oecd.org/dataoecd/21/15/41278761.pdf

12. http://www.guardian.co.uk/education/2010/jun/09/david-willetts-students-tuition-fees

13. http://www.slc.co.uk/statistics/facts%20and%20%20figures/take_up_stats_9105.html

14. http://www.parliament.uk/documents/commons/lib/research/rp2007/rp07-078.pdf

15. N.C. O'Leary and P.J. Sloane, 'The Changing Wage Return to an Undergraduate Education', Discussion Paper No. 1549, Institute for the Study of Labour (IZA), March 2005, cited in Nick Bosanquet and Blair Gibbs, 'The iPod Generation', *Reform*, 2005, p. 27.

16. The *Economist* reported that arts graduates can expect to be paid 4 per cent less over their lifetime than someone without any degree at all.

17. Barbara Gunnell and Martin Bright, 'Creative Survival in Hard Times', New Deal of the Mind, 2010, p. 12.

18. 'Unleashing Aspiration: The Final Report of the Panel on Fair Access to the Professions', HMSO, July 2009.

19. Low Pay Commission findings and a milkround survey of 300 students, which found that the majority of young people think internships matter. One is quoted as saying: 'There are plenty of graduates with the right qualifications, but doing an internship shows you're not only capable of doing the job, but you're enthusiastic enough to work without pay in the field in which you're interested.'

20. All activities described on 'Interns Anonymous' website.

21. Gunnell and Bright, 'Creative Survival in Hard Times', p. 21.

22. The only nod you get to this from the government is on that Talent Pool website, which gives a link to minimum wage guidance.

23. In 2009, intern Nicola Vetta, with the help of her union BECTU, took film company London Dreams Motion Pictures to an employment tribunal in Reading because they had refused to pay her expenses. The tribunal's decision came as a shock. They ruled that it was illegal for anyone to be interning. If people are engaged in meaningful work, then they are entitled to the minimum wage. Don't stand for it!

24. 'National Minimum Wage: Low Pay Commission Report', HMSO, 2010, pp. 108–10.

25. See 'Job Mobility and Job Tenure in the UK' by Claire Macaulay, Labour Market Division, Office for National Statistics, November 2003.

26. Paul Gregg and Jonathan Wadsworth, 'Mind the Gap, Please: The Changing Nature of Entry Jobs in Britain', *Economica*, Vol. 67, No. 268, November 2000, pp. 499–524, p. 502.

27. http://www.tuc.org.uk/ontheedge/facts.cfm?theme=ontheedge

28. 'Understanding First Time Buyers', Council of Mortgage Lenders, 2005, p. 49.

29. The OECD define low pay as two thirds of median pay.

30. Gregg and Wadsworth, 'Mind the Gap, Please', p. 518.

31. Disposable income of the lowest 10 per cent was only 2.8 times less than that of the richest 10 per cent in 1977. By 2002 that figure was four times less. Institute of Fiscal Studies, 'Distribution of Real Household Income', cited in *Social Trends*, 34, Office for National Statistics, 2004, Figure 5.14.

32. This rise in inequality between generations is made worse by the high tax burden of young people in full-time work. For example, young graduates have an effective tax burden of 47.6 per cent. See Bosanquet and Gibbs, 'The iPOD Generation', *Reform*, 2005.

33. 'Growing Unequal? Income Distribution and Poverty in OECD Countries', OECD Publishing, October 2008.

34. In fact they're unlikely to get those hours. So, assuming they worked 45 hours a week and took full holiday entitlement, they would get paid only £8,260 a year, 60 per cent of what they would need to be independent on the bare minimum. The same calculation for an under-21-year-old would be £11,161, or 80 per cent of the bare minimum.

35. Simone Melis et al., 'Monitoring the Impact of the National Minimum Wage: A Report for the Low Pay Commission', Incomes Data Services, March 2009, p. 10.

36. Peter Levell, Richard May, Cormac O'Dea and David Phillips, 'A Survey of the UK Benefit System', Institute for Fiscal Studies, December 2009.

37. Ibid.

38. http://www.crisis.org.uk/data/files/publications/26070810 HousingBenefitsnotBarriersFINAL.pdf

39. *Breakthrough Britain: Dynamic Benefits, Towards Welfare that Works*, Centre for Social Justice, 2009, p. 20.

40. A few years later he became a member of the Bank of England's Monetary Policy Committee when Gordon Brown gave independence to the Bank of England.

41. Quoted from *Pandora's Box*, Adam Curtis, BBC, 1993.

42. Shiv Malik, 'A Very British Sickness', *New Statesman*, 10 January 2005.

43. Craig Lindsay, 'A Century of Labour Market Change: 1900 to 2000', Labour Market Division, Office for National Statistics, March 2003.

44. Labour Market Division, Office for National Statistics, April 2010, p. 4.

45. Cited in Nick Bosanquet, Blair Gibbs, Seth Cumming and Andrew Halden, 'Class of 2006: A Lifebelt for the iPod Generation', *Reform*, September 2006, p. 13.

46. Gordon Brown, Jeremy Paxman interview, *Newsnight*, BBC2, 30 April 2010.

47. 'Income and Source of Income 1970–2008', Family Spending Survey, Office for National Statistics, table A47.

48. http://www.oecd.org/dataoecd/27/1/38796126.pdf, June 2007.

49. Marco Francescone and Katrin Golsch, 'The Process of Globalization and Transitions to Adulthood in Britain', in *Globalization, Uncertainty and Youth in Society*, edited by Hans-Peter Blossfeld, Routledge, 2005, pp. 249–76.

50. Federal Reserve Board chairman Alan Greenspan, 'Ideas and Economic Value', address to The Economic Club of Chicago, 19 October 1995.

51. Marco Francescone and Katrin Golsch, 'The Process of Globalization and Transitions to Adulthood in Britain', pp. 249–76.

52. Richard Sennett, *Corrosion of Character: The Personal Consequences of Work in the New Capitalism*, New York: W.W. Norton, 1998, p. 26.

53. http://www.oecd.org/document/9/0,3343, en_2649_201185_41530009_1_1_1_1,00.html

Chapter 3: Inheritance

1. See ukpollingreport.co.uk/blog/archives/1045 for an excellent summary.
2. … though it's not a great piece of writing. Notice how Osborne also said that home-owners 'have the threat of inheritance tax hanging over them' – that's a classic piece of double-talk. Inheritance tax is paid by the living, not the 'home-owners' who in this case would be, er, dead. You can see here that Osborne is appealing not to the young people who will inherit but to the baby boomers who want to leave a meaningful inheritance.
3. Office for National Statistics release, April 2010.
4. OECD, *Economic Outlook*, 86, November 2009.
5. 'Long-term Public Finance Report: An Analysis of Fiscal Sustainability', HM Treasury, 2009, p. 42.
6. http://press.helptheaged.org.uk/_press/Releases/_items/Pensions_not_pin_money_report.htm
7. http://www.equalities.gov.uk/media/press_releases/age_consultation.aspx
8. http://www.telegraph.co.uk/finance/markets/ftse100/6924041/Third-of-FTSE-companies-plan-pension-liabilities-cut.html
9. *Public Expenditure Statistical Analyses* (PESA) 2009, published June 2009.
10. Interview with Martin Weale.
11. They're surprisingly good company, actually.
12. http://news.bbc.co.uk/1/hi/health/7710380.stm
13. Nick Bosanquet and Blair Gibbs, 'The iPOD Generation', *Reform*, 2005, p. 9.
14. 'Long-term Public Finance Report', HM Treasury, 2009, p. 9.
15. Ibid., p. 45.
16. PFI was specifically used by Gordon Brown as a way of keeping debt off the government's balance sheet in order to satisfy the golden rules he created as chancellor.

17. Cited in http://www.monbiot.com/archives/2009/05/26/the-real-expenses-scandal, and others

18. http://www.guardian.co.uk/commentisfree/2007/sep/04/comment.politics

19. Statistics drawn from 'PFI Signed Projects List', HM Treasury, February 2010.

20. Half the total is due after 2020.

21. Check out the committee's 63rd report, HM Treasury, 'Tendering and Benchmarking in PFI', for a particularly gruesome analysis of government's failure to get value for money from PFI.

22. C. Hagist, S. Moog, B. Raffelhuschen, J. Vatter, 'Public Debt and Demography – An International Comparison Using Generational Accounting', CESifo DICE report, April 2009.

23. Ibid., Figure 2, p. 33.

24. Ibid., p. 34.

25. Martin Weale, 'The Burden of the National Debt', *National Institute Economic Review*, No. 210, October 2009, p. 5.

26. Letter to John Taylor, 1816.

27. Letter to James Madison, 1789.

28. Article I, Section 27.

29. Article L 110b al 1, as cited in Axel Gosseries, 'On Future Generations' Future Rights', *The Journal of Political Philosophy*, Vol. 126, No. 4, December 2008, p. 448.

30. See Zac Goldsmith's *The Constant Economy*, London: Atlantic Books, pp. 93–105, for a précis of the tragedy of overfishing.

31. HSBC study into the right to buy, December 2009.

32. Office for National Statistics figures on share ownership, historical series.

33. http://www.telegraph.co.uk/finance/personalfinance/7086997/Individual-share-ownership-falls-to-all-time-low.html

34. OECD Factbook, 2009.

35. Stephen B. Bond, 'UK Investment and the Capital Market', Institute for Fiscal Studies and Nuffield College, Oxford, 2001, p. 4.
36. HM Treasury, *Planning Sustainable Public Spending: Lessons from Previous Policy Experience*, 2000, p. 2.
37. Net saving is net disposable income less final consumption expenditure.
38. Weale, 'The Burden of the National Debt', p. 7.
39. Ray Barrell and Martin Weale, 'Fiscal Policy, Fairness Between Generations and National Saving', National Institute of Economic and Social Research, June 2009, p. 14.
40. Interview with Martin Weale.

Chapter 4: Politics

1. Most significant was perhaps Twitter, the microblogging site, which broadcast the ill-judged comments of several candidates, forcing their resignations, and was used by almost every political party to relay information and spin lines about every tiny twist in the campaign.
2. http://www.guardian.co.uk/politics/blog/2010/apr/23/michael-white-leaders-debate-british-politics-changed
3. Dunbabin Road polling station in the Wavertree constituency, Liverpool, ran out of ballots. Many more locked voters out.
4. Conversation with local Labour organiser.
5. http://www.independent.co.uk/news/uk/politics/bank-of-england-governor-poll-winner-will-be-out-of-power-for-a-generation-1958867.html
6. David Cameron, 'We will tackle Labour's legacy of debt', email to supporters, 7 June 2010.
7. David Cameron, 'Our ageing population', 23 October 2006.
8. David Cameron, 'Young Adult Trust will make a constructive difference', 30 October 2006.
9. http://www.independent.co.uk/news/uk/politics/labour-and-tories-target-the-baby-boomers-420874.html

10. David Willetts and Frank Field, 'Should Baby Boomers Feel the Pinch?', *Standpoint*, March 2010.

11. Ipsos MORI, 'How Britain Voted in 2010', 21 May 2010. Base: 10,211 GB adults aged 18+ (of which 5,927 were 'absolutely certain to vote' or said they had already voted), interviewed 19 March–5 May 2010.

12. http://www.newstatesman.com/life-and-society/2007/03/generation-pensions-housing; so small wonder that in the month before the 2010 election, 30 per cent of young people told pollsters that they didn't believe their vote would count.

13. http://www.independent.co.uk/news/uk/politics/labour-and-tories-target-the-baby-boomers-420874.html

14. Quoted in *The Neophiliacs* by Christopher Booker, London: Collins, 1969, p. 101.

15. Ibid., p. 23.

16. Ibid., p. 23.

17. Tariq Ali, 'Where Has All the Rage Gone?', *Guardian*, 27 March 2008.

18. Paul Johnson, 'The Menace of Beatlism', *New Statesman*, 28 February 1964.

19. Harold Wilson, *The New Britain*, London: Penguin Books, 1964, pp. 130–2.

20. Tariq Ali, *Street Fighting Years*, London: Verso, 2005, p. 7.

21. Germaine Greer, 'Mozic and the Revolution', *Oz*, 24, October 1969.

22. In fact, this narrative begins long after the idea of 'individualism' finds modern expression. The philosophy of the 'individual' was fundamental to much 18th- and 19th-century political philosophy. Adam Smith was an advocate of economic individualism. Jeremy Bentham's utilitarianism rests on the observation that no individual can claim that their own happiness counts for any more or less than another's. J.S. Mill, de Tocqueville, Nietzsche and Marx hedge much of their thinking around the role of the individual and the systems

that can be created to ensure that each can express or fulfil themselves to the greatest extent possible.

23. The number of sixth-formers doubled in the decade following the Butler Education Act of 1944, and the number of school-leavers aged fifteen or over also doubled between 1955 and 1965. See John Street, *Youth Culture, 20th Century Britain: Economic, Social and Cultural Change*, ed. Paul Johnson, London: Longman, 1994, p. 463.

24. The quest for self-expression does not, of course, begin in the 1940s – it goes back to the Enlightenment, when the very definition of an individual and his or her place in society becomes the subject of the first truly modern thinkers.

25. Mark Abrams, *The Teenage Consumer*, London: Press Exchange, 1959, p. 19.

26. The teenage consumers had unique patterns of consumption: they made up 44 per cent of all record sales and record player sales, 26 per cent of cinema admissions, 24 per cent of cosmetics sales, 19 per cent of footwear sales, and 16 per cent of women's clothing sales. Their spending was only 6 per cent of the whole of consumer spending.

27. Richard Hoggart, *The Uses of Literacy*, New Jersey: Transaction Publishers, 3rd edn, 2004, p. 265 (first published in 1957 by Essential Books).

28. Ibid., p. 222.

29. Institute of Life Insurance, *Finance-Related Attitudes of Youth*, 1970, and *Youth*, 1974. Both available in the Daniel Yankelovich Papers held at the Thomas J. Dodd Research Center, University of Connecticut, 56:1341 and 56:1342.

30. Interview with Adam Curtis, *The Century of the Self*, Part 3, 'There is a Policeman Inside Our Heads: He Must be Destroyed', BBC2, 31 March 2002.

31. *Youth*, 1974, p. 59.

32. Ibid., p. 64.

33. Examples of VALs questions include: 'Just as the Bible says, the world literally was created in six days.' 'I love to make things I can use every day.' 'I am very interested in how mechanical things, such as engines, work.' 'I would like to understand more about how the universe works.' Things have moved on quite a bit since then – with consumers' demographics, psychological profile, location, income and spending habits all weighed in mind-bending detail. See *No Logo* by Naomi Klein (Flamingo, 2000), or just look at your Tesco Clubcard, which, along with systems like ACORN and MOSAIC, can provide 'geodemographic segmentation analysis' – where people live, what they tend to buy, where and why.

34. Naomi Klein talks a great deal about this in *No Logo*, and examples of this kind of advertising are everywhere – just turn on your TV and think about the product or service and how it's being advertised to you.

35. Quoted from Curtis, *The Century of the Self*, Part 4, 'Eight People Sipping Wine in Kettering', BBC2, 7 April 2002.

36. From Bo Sarlvik and Ivor Crewe, *Decade of Dealignment: The Conservative Victory of 1979 and Electoral Trends in the 1970s*, Cambridge University Press, 1983.

37. Author interview by telephone, March 2010.

38. Margaret Thatcher, interview with Douglas Keay, 'Aids, Education and the Year 2000!', *Woman's Own*, 31 October 1987.

39. Cited in David Harvey, *A Brief History of Neoliberalism*, Oxford University Press, 2005, p. 20.

40. Milton Friedman and Rose D. Friedman, *Free to Choose*, New York: Harcourt Brace, 1980, p. 147.

41. Interview with Simon Webley, 4 June 1986, by Radhika Desai, professor at the Department of Political Studies, University of Manitoba, published in her paper, 'Second-Hand Dealers in

Ideas: Think-Tanks and Thatcherite Hegemony', in *New Left Review*, I/203, 1994.

42. 'The bureaucracy can manipulate the agenda for legislative action for the purpose of securing outcomes favourable to its own interests. The bureaucracy can play off one set of constituents against others, insuring that budgets rise much beyond plausible efficiency limits.' See James M. Buchanan, 'Politics without Romance: A Sketch of Positive Public Choice Theory and its Normative Implications', in James M. Buchanan and Robert D. Tollison, eds, *The Theory of Public Choice – II*, Ann Arbor: University of Michigan Press, 1984.

43. James M. Buchanan and Gordon Tullock, *The Calculus of Consent*, Ann Arbor: University of Michigan Press, Ann Arbor Paperbacks, 1965, p. 47.

44. http://www.ipeg.org.uk/papers/Ch5_John_Johnson_FINAL_(2).pdf, p. 109.

45. Buchanan, 'Politics without Romance', p. 11.

46. Also worth noting here is the work of Al Enthoven, the former Cold War ballistic missile first-strike strategist hired by Thatcher to shake up the NHS.

47. http://news.bbc.co.uk/onthisday/hi/dates/stories/july/22/newsid_2516000/2516139.stm

48. Tony Blair, 'Give Britain back its sense of purpose', Labour election broadcast, April 1997.

49. Tony Blair, speech to Labour party conference, 1999.

50. http://www.epolitix.com/latestnews/article-detail/newsarticle/tony-blair-social-exclusion-speech-in-full/?no_cache=1

51. Tony Blair, speech to Progressive Government conference, 2003.

52. Susan Mayor, 'Hospitals take short-term measures to meet targets', *British Medical Journal*, 326:1054, 17 May 2003.

53. Independent inquiry into care provided by Mid Staffordshire NHS Foundation Trust, January 2005–March 2009, Volume 1, p. 25.

54. In *The Triumph of the Political Class* (Simon & Schuster, 2007), Peter Oborne defines 'modernisers' as those who 'do not subscribe to the core beliefs that bind their organisations together'.

55. The group included Peter Mandelson, Tony Blair and Alastair Campbell.

56. To give just one example of how these techniques were manifested: one of the first acts they undertook following Tony Blair's victory in the Labour leadership battle was to rebrand the party as 'New Labour'.

57. Interviewed in Adam Curtis, *The Century of the Self*, Part 4, 'Eight People Sipping Wine in Kettering', BBC2, 7 April 2002.

58. Quoted from Robert M. Worcester and Paul R. Baines, 'Two Triangulation Models in Political Marketing: The Market Positioning Analogy', Elections on the Horizon conference, British Library, London, 15 March 2004.

59. Quoted in Dennis Kavanagh, 'Party Democracy and Political Marketing: No Place for Amateurs?', paper presented at the Political Communications in the Global World conference, Mainz, 30–31 October 2003.

60. Philip Gould, 'The mission remains the same', BBC website, 23 February 2000.

61. Philip Gould, 'What "permanent campaign"?', BBC News, 21 November 2002.

62. Interviewed in Adam Curtis, *The Century of the Self*, Part 4, 'Eight People Sipping Wine in Kettering', BBC2, 7 April 2002.

63. Geoff Mulgan, *Good and Bad Power*, Chapter 15, 'Service to the Future', London: Penguin, 2006, p. 306.

64. Derek Scott, *Financial Times*, 5 June 2005; quoted in Oborne, *The Triumph of the Political Class*.

65. See Gary Becker and George Stigler, 'De Gustibus Non est Disputandum', *American Economic Review*, 67(2), 1977, pp. 76–90.

66. Brian J. Gibbs, 'Inward Decision Making: Chameleonic Consumers and the Self-Manipulation of Tastes', working paper, Melbourne Business School, University of Melbourne, 20 September 2005, pp. 5, 14.

67. When everyone was asked to predict how displeasing another twenty doses would be, those who expected to actually have another twenty doses felt less averse towards repeat tastings than those who were told they had to taste the solution only once.

68. Gibbs, 'Inward Decision Making', p. 5.

69. Cited in George Loewenstein, Daniel Read and Roy Baumesiter (eds), *Time and Decision: Economic and Psychological Perspectives on Intertemporal Choice*, New York: Russell Sage Foundation, 2003, p. 366.

70. See Brian Wansink and Kim Junyong, 'Bad Popcorn in Big Buckets: Portion Size Can Influence Consumption as Much as Taste', *Journal of Nutrition, Education and Behaviour*, Vol. 37, No. 5, 2005, pp. 242–5.

71. Loewenstein et al, *Time and Decision*, p. 368.

72. Ibid., p. 382.

73. Cass Sunstein and Richard Thaler, *Nudge*, Yale University Press, 2008, p. 5.

74. It's no surprise that the new prime minister of Great Britain and Northern Ireland used to work in PR.

75. Tony Blair, speech to Labour party conference, September 2004.

76. Kavanagh, 'Party Democracy and Political Marketing', p. 2.

77. John Marshall, 'Membership of UK Political Parties', House of Commons Library, 17 August 2009, p. 3.

78. http://www.dailymail.co.uk/news/article-1183455/Blair-gurus-girl-Georgia-Gould-22-loses-fight-safe-seat.html

79. If you wondered why Nick Clegg and David Cameron seemed to get on so well following the 2010 election victory, their

membership of the political class may provide some of the answer.

Conclusion

1. Shiv has an addiction for Googling 'jilted generation'.
2. Richard Garner, 'Summer of Discontent: 69 graduates for every job vacancy', *Independent*, 6 July 2010.
3. Vernon Coaker, '50.4 per cent of pupils in the maintained sector achieved five or more GCSEs at grade A*–C, including English and maths; substantial rise in maintained schools' GCSE results', Department for Children, Families and Schools, media release, 15 October 2009. These figures suggest that in 2009 around 300,000 children left school without the basic requirements demanded by employers and universities.
4. Pre-recession figures from the Global Entrepreneurship Monitor show that Britain has a Total Entrepreneurial Activity (TEA) level of 6.3 per cent, while those of the USA, Australia and New Zealand are roughly twice that figure. In the USA, the 25–34 age group is the most entrepreneurial at 17.3 per cent. The equivalent figure for the UK is 6.9 per cent. Quoted in Nick Bosanquet and Blair Gibbs, 'The iPod Generation', *Reform*, 2005, p. 21.
5. For a full list of MPs' expenses claims, see the *Daily Telegraph* website.
6. David Hume, 'Of the Origin of Government', in *The Philosophical Works of David Hume*, Vol. 2, Book 3, Part 2, Little, Brown, 1754, p. 311.
7. The complete quote from 'Of the Origin of Government' is: 'Magistrates find an immediate interest in the interest of any considerable part of their subjects. They need consult nobody but themselves to form any scheme for the promoting of that interest. And as the failure of any one piece in the execution is connected, though not immediately, with the failure of the whole, they prevent that failure, because they find no

interest in it, either immediate or remote. Thus bridges are built; harbours opened; ramparts raised; canals formed; fleets equipped; and armies disciplined everywhere, by the care of government, which, though composed of men subject to all human infirmities, becomes, by one of the finest and most subtle inventions imaginable, a composition, which is, in some measure, exempted from all these infirmities.'

8. Margaret Thatcher, speech to Scottish Conservative party conference, 12 May 1979.

9. Tony Blair, speech to Labour supporters, Royal Festival Hall, 2 May 1997.

10. It's arguable that education to sixteen is a 'right', since it's codified in law (Local Education Act, 1944), but this happened long before Tony Blair came along.

11. Bad house-building is a perennial problem in Britain – check out the regular TV shows that feature *Britain's Worst Builders* (ITV), *Britain's Bad Housing* (Channel 4), and the hundreds of press reports written in the last decade regarding poor home-build standards.

12. The average number of houses built between 1951 and 1980 was 321,000 per year. The average builds per year for 1999–2009 was 191,000. The difference is 131,000 homes per year. So the total shortfall is around 1.44 million missing homes over the last eleven years. What does it cost to build a social home? Well, the figure that seems reasonable is £50 per square foot or £450 per square metre. The average home is around 85m². We take a lower figure to reflect social housing: 80m². This means that the cost to build a house is around £36,000 per dwelling – excluding land cost. So 1.44 million × £36,000 = £51.8 billion.

13. There's much that could help London Citizens and others like them in the government's proposals for Community Housing Trusts, which give local areas the ability to deliver land for

housing quickly. But, until the fine detail of any legislation is known, it's difficult to predict how successful this might be.

14. Will Davies, *Reinventing the Firm*, Demos, 2009, p. 69.
15. Joseph Lampel, Ajay Bhalla and Pushkar Jha, 'Model Growth: Do employee-owned businesses deliver sustainable performance?', Cass Business School, January 2010. The survey was based on an in-depth survey of senior executives and analysis of the financial data of over 250 companies.

Acknowledgements

This book would never have happened without the advice, wisdom, and hard work of a long list of benevolent people. And, while it goes without saying that any errors that remain in the text are the sole responsibility of the authors, it's also worth pointing out that the book may never have happened in the first place without the help of others. They include Simon Flynn who first took a punt on the book, and Najma Finlay, Andrew Furlow and Duncan Heath who have all put up with our tardiness. We must also thank Tom Boylston who burned the midnight oil with us on several nerve-racking nights before deadline, and Jim Cranshaw who was always ready with instant and perspicacious analysis. Further, we owe a debt to the documentary-maker Adam Curtis whose programmes and good advice at the start of this process dramatically improved our ideas. The list of those who have offered encouragement, support and guidance in various forms includes our families, Meghan Benton, Emily Best, Andy Bradford, Martin Bright, Sarah Broadhurst, Paul and Linda Carter, Ben Chu, Emma Crowe, Foad Dizadji-Bahmani, Alan Evans, Claire Fox, Peter Gerard, John Hills, Carys Hughes, Tim Minogue, Fraser Nelson, Margareta Pagano, Jon Plackett, Tyne and J.S. Rafaeli, Adam Ramsey, Anna Tamas, Martin Weale, Danielle Williams and all at Foyles Bookshop.

Finally, there's no way any of this would have come about without the saintly patience and Thatcher-like determination of our remarkable wives Julia and Miriam. Though it might not be saying much given all that's come before, we will always be in your debt.